Fall of the Philippines

D1549979

Ward Rutherford

Fall of the Philippines

Editor-in-Chief: Barrie Pitt
Editor: David Mason
Art Director: Sarah Kingham
Picture Editor: Robert Hunt
Designer: David Allen
Cover: Denis Piper
Special Drawings: John Batchelor
Photographic Research: Jonathan Moore
Cartographer: Richard Natkiel

Photographs for this book were specially selected from the following Archives: from left to right pages 8-9 US Army; 10 US National Archives; 10-13 US Army; 13 Keystone; 14-15 Imperial War Museum; 16 US Army; 16 IWM; 17 US Army; 17 US National Archives; 17 US Army; 22 Keystone; 23 US Marine Corps; 26-27 Keystone; 29 Fuji; 29 US Navy; 33 IWM; 33 Martin Caidin; 34-35 US National Archives; 36-37 Fuji; 38 US Army; 38-39 US Navy; 40 IWM; 41 Fuji; 42-43 Yap; 45-46 US National Archives; 48-49 Yap; 50-51 Fuji; 52-53 US Navy; 52-53 Keystone; 54 US National Archives; 54 US Navy; 54 US Army; 54 US Navy; 56 Keystone; 57 US Army; US National Archives; 60-61 Yap; 62 Fuji; 63 US Army; 66 Yap; 66-67 Keystone; 70-71 Fuji; 70 Keystone; 74 Yap; 76-79 Fuji; 80-81 US Army; 81-83 US National Archives; 84-89 Fuji; 90 Yap; 91-92 Fuji; 93-95 Yap; 96-97 US Marine Corps; 100-101 Fuji; 104 US National Archives; 105 Keystone; 106-107 Yap; 108-113 US Army; 117 Fuji; 120-121 US Army; 122 US National Archives; 122 US Army; 123 Keystone; 126-127 Fuji; 128 Yap; 129 US Army; 130 Keystone; 131 Yap; 131 Keystone; 132 Fuji; 138-145 Yap; 144-145 US Army; 146 US Marines; 146 US National Archives; 142 Yap; 147 Fuji; 148 Yap; 149 US Army; 149 Fuji; 152-153 Keystone; 156 US Airforce; 156-157 US Army; 157-158 Yap; 159 US National Archives; Front cover US Navy; Back cover Keystone
The publishers wish to extend special thanks to Dr Diosdado M Yap, Editor-Publisher, Bataan Magazine, Washington DC for his permission to reproduce certain photographs from his collection

First U.S. Printing: October, 1971
First Pan/Ballantine Printing: August, 1972

Printed in the United States of America
Ballantine Books, Ltd.—An Intertext Publisher
Pan Books, Ltd.
33 Tothill Street, London, S.W. 1

Contents

The Onslaught

Introduction by Barrie Pitt.

The conquest of the Philippines was only a part of a much larger strategic design, given by the Japanese the grandiose title of the 'Great East Asia War'. This included the invasion of Malaya, Thailand, Borneo, and the Dutch East Indies.

Committed since 1937 to a war in China, Japan desperately needed oil to fuel her aircraft and military vehicles, and many other essential raw materials to feed the capacious maw of her munitions industry; and in 1940 and 1941 she found her sources of such essential commodities were being removed one by one.

Firstly, an iron embargo had been imposed on her by America; then she lost her supplies of rubber, abruptly cut off by the British; then in July, 1941, her assets in the United States were frozen and her all-important imports of American oil ceased immediately. Japan had to make a choice: either to abandon her military gains in China or to take steps to obtain those essential materials by force of arms. There was oil in Borneo, Java, Sumatra which would satisfy her present needs, with yet another source available further north in Burma, and Malaya could provide her with rubber. However, to protect her shipping-lanes and to provide a staging-post for her further conquests, Japan must also seize the American-controlled Philippines. The effect of all these courses of action must inevitably be to challenge the strength of Britain and the United States. Although Britain was embroiled in a war in Europe, America was as yet uncommitted, despite the restrictions she had imposed on the sale of raw materials to Japan.

On 6th December, 1941, the Japanese created the Southern Army under General Count Hisaichi Terauchi for the specific purpose of annexing the essential sources of mineral wealth, together with such other territory as was necessary to the achievement of the basic objectives. The Army was composed of ten divisions and three mixed brigades and for the capture of the Philippines alone, Terauchi assigned two full divisions (the 16th and 48th), two tank regiments, two regiments and one battalion of medium artillery, three engineering regiments and five anti-aircraft battalions, altogether making up the 14th Army commanded by Lieutenant-General Masaharu Homma. They would face a defensive force consisting of ten infantry divisions.

Japanese preparations for the assault on the Philippines were typically thorough. From the mid-'thirties onwards they had carried out espionage activities on a large scale, and their intelligence appreciation of the forces which would oppose them was comprehensive. As a result, and having learned the value of air power from their experiences in China, they made available for the assault two air forces to support their ground attacks; the 5th Air Group of the Army Air Force with 3075 aircraft, and the 11th Air Fleet (both land and carrier based) of the Japanese navy; 444 aircraft. The air attacks would go in at dawn on the 7th December 1941 (though they would occur some three hours later than the Pearl Harbor attack due to difference in longitude) and in the event, on the first day of battle they lost only seven aircraft while destroying eighteen out of thirty-four American B17 bombers, plus two-thirds of the American fighter strength.

On the 10th December the army divisions began the first landings.

General Douglas MacArthur, who commanded USAFFE (United States Army Forces in the Far East), an integrated force combining the old Philippine Department with the forces of the Philippine Commonwealth, had taken up his appointment in May, 1941. Rejecting the defensive nature of 'Rainbow V', a war plan drawn up in consultation with the British General Staff and designed for a situation in which America was fighting both Japan and Germany, he suggested that his growing forces should be used to keep the Japanese out of the Philippines altogether, and, provided his air strength was increased, he thought that an aggressive use of air power would seriously incommode the Japanese plans of conquest by threatening their sea lines-of-communication. To his delight, General Marshall approved of these ideas and reinforcements were sent to MacArthur's command, although they did not arrive in the numbers he thought necessary. By the time war started he had, in numbers at least, a far stronger force than the compilers of War Plan Orange III – precrusor of Rainbow V – had envisaged when they first formulated their plans for the defence of the islands.

But when war came, and despite MacArthur's accurate prediction of the landing areas the Japanese would use, plus intelligence reports of a large convoy of troop transports heading for the Philippines received two days before the main landings took place on 2nd December, the defenders were still not prepared, and the only real obstacle to hamper the assault troops was the rough sea which made the handling of their barges difficult. By 23rd December, MacArthur had decide to revert to war plan Rainbow V and concentrated his troops in the more easily defensible area of Bataan and on the island of Corregidor at the entrance to Manila Bay.

As a result, although there was truth in General Homma's contention that the Allied retreat in the Bataan Peninsula resembled 'a cat going into a bag' it took three months of savage and bitter fighting, from early January to April, before General King surrendered his exhausted and disease-ridden troops to the almost equally exhausted Japanese.

Once the forces on Bataan had surrendered, it was only a matter of time before Corregidor must fall. Battered by huge Japanese siege guns – 240-mm howitzers – and with no means of replenishing stores, the situation of the 15,000 Americans on the island was hopeless. A beach-head was established by the Japanese on 5th May and on 6th May, 1942, Corregidor surrendered to a landing force of only 1000 men and the garrison followed their comrades from Bataan into cruel captivity.

The loss of the Philippines was a sad blow to American prestige and illustrated the fundamental difference between the combatants – on the American side confusion, disorganisation, and a lack of decision amongst the leaders; on the Japanese side sound training, discipline, and confidence in ultimate victory and in the rightness of their cause.

The difference between a nation prepared for war, and one which hoped that war would pass it by.

Rumours of War

During the summer and autumn of 1941 they were saying that war might come to the Philippines. But along its palmy shores the Pacific lapped in white fringes of foam. The extravagantly shaped, brilliantly coloured butterflies weaved among the hibiscus and bougainvillea, the jasmine and the wild orchids. In the plantations the fruit ripened: mangoes, guava, breadfruit, papaya, tamarind, bananas, pineapples and coconuts. In the trees the birds squawked and on the rocks and dry walls the lizards, of which a hundred species are to be found in the islands, sunned themselves.

The people, largely Catholic from the days of Spanish occupation, but with an admixture of some four per cent of Muslims descended from earlier Arab conquerors, went about their daily tasks as peaceably as any people on earth.

Who could feel belligerent towards such a place and such a people?

A mixture of Malay, Chinese, Japanese, Hindu, Arab and Spaniard, which produced happy-hearted men and beautiful women, the Filipinos were at that time feeling their way uncertainly towards independence from their occupier, the United States

American forces march through Manila prior to Pearl Harbor

Above: Manuel Quezon. *Right:* the occupying US army parades

of America, which had seized their islands at the turn of the century, from the collapsing Spanish empire.

Of more concern to the Filipinos that year than the distant possibility of war were their own local politics. Excitement and tension was building up for the elections which were to take place in November, the first under the amended constitution. This had established a two-tier form of government, with a Senate, elected by national vote, and a House of Representatives, chosen by district voting. It also provided for a four-year term of office for both president and vice-president.

Such freedom as the Philippines had so far enjoyed, and which allowed them to elect their own president and legislature, was the result of a bill passed by both Houses of the American Congress and ratified by the President in 1934. Under its terms the Philippines would have full independence in ten years.

The negotiations which resulted in this bill had thrown up at least one political figure of eminence. This was Manuel Quezon, who, in 1935, became the first President of the Philippine Commonwealth – as it was then called – with another leading local politician, Sergio Osmena, as his vice-president.

One question which had proved particularly difficult in the negotiations was the presence in the islands of the United States bases. The Filipinos had objected so strongly to this military presence that their legislature had rejected an earlier independence bill. For the present the question was in abeyance, but it was widely believed that the Americans would leave when the Philippines' own forces had reached the point at which they could reasonably be expected to take over responsibility for the area themselves.

For the American soldiers, sailors and airmen who manned the bases or were assisting in the training of the Philippine Army, there was about

10

their existence a lotus-eating atmosphere, partly the product of the humid enervating climate, and partly of the knowledge that they were in a place whose life as an American base was nearing its end. There were some officers who insisted that war might come at any moment, and emphasized the need to prepare for it. But most of the time the men, like soldiers everywhere, carried out their routines with a minimum of effort.

In their spare time they explored the interior, with its burnt-out volcanoes or Nipa-palm villages, where the primitive tribes lived as they had lived for centuries. The visitors would buy pieces of local pottery or Ifugao woodcarving to take home. When they were not exploring they dated the fascinating local girls – half-Oriental, half-Occidental – or fished the rich lakes, watched *jai-alai* games, swam in the lagoons or lazed on the beaches. Sometimes they laughed at the antics of the saucer-eyed tarsiers or caught a glimpse of a 'Robber' crab as it climbed a coconut palm, clipped off a nut and husked it with a big, sharp claw.

And all the time they wondered which of them would be lucky enough to spend Christmas at home.

Wars, they believed, were not fought among the profuse and violent colours of tropical landscapes. They were fought under the lowering, rainy skies of Europe, in the mud of Russia, or the burning deserts of North Africa.

Crisis Approaches

There had been something almost dynastic about the appointment of a MacArthur as military adviser to the Government of the Philippine Commonwealth, with the rank of field-marshal in their army. For, in March 1899 Douglas MacArthur's father, General Arthur MacArthur, had led the American forces which defeated the Filipino insurgents and captured Manila to mark the start of American occupation.

But his son had more than hereditary claims. His association with the Philippines went back to his first tour of duty, in 1904, just after he had graduated from West Point Military Academy. Then, in the mid-1920s,

Douglas MacArthur, now a major-general, had made a second visit, this time as commander of the Philippine Department, the branch of the army responsible for the islands' defence.

At that time also the young lawyer Quezon was emerging as leader of his people in their struggle for complete home rule. So, it was logical that in 1935 Quezon should go to MacArthur, now Chief of Staff in Washington, and invite him to undertake the building of a defence force for the Commonwealth. In the autumn of that year he

Below and right: the Filipino army, under MacArthur's guidance, prepares for war

had sailed for Manila yet again to undertake his new task, knowing that with the American units already in the islands and the small British and Dutch forces in Borneo, Malaya, and the East Indies, his were the only bulwarks against Japan. (Like Quezon and the General Staff in Washington, he regarded the Japanese as the principal threat to peace in the area).

For his defence force he envisaged an army of citizen-soldiers based on the Swiss model. They would be backed by a small regular, professional force which initially would consist of the Philippine Constabulary, an American unit already in the islands. Under this plan the Commonwealth would, upon full independence in 1946, have some forty divisions, making up, in all, about 400,000 men, who would be stationed at strategic points throughout the islands.

In carrying out the task MacArthur, as well as Quezon, expected heavy American support. When it became clear this would not be forthcoming on the scale they had hoped for relations between Manila and Washington grew so strained that in July 1938 MacArthur resigned his American army commission.

In May 1941, however, he received a letter from his successor as Chief of Staff in Washington, General George Marshall, inviting him to take on a

The Japanese War Cabinet with Prime Minister Tojo

can oil on which the Japanese depended for their war against the Chinese.

Japan's moderate prime minister, Prince Fumimaro Konoye, resigned after his attempts at negotiation failed and his place was taken by the former War Minister, General Hideki Tojo, a known militarist. It was now obvious that the scale pan was bearing ominously down toward war.

Over many years, Washington had developed for the defence of the Philippines a whole series of plans. These were identified by colour-codes, each colour representing a different situation. The latest of these had been devised in the spring of 1941 and was called 'War Plan Orange III' or 'WPO-III' for short. It was intended to cover a situation in which only Japan and America were involved in war.

It postulated the abandonment of Manila and the withdrawal of the defenders to Bataan Peninsula, overlooking Manila Bay. From here and from the offshore fortresses, of which Corregidor was the most important, the bay could be defended until such time as the Pacific Fleet, 5,000 miles away at Pearl Harbor, could arrive on the scene.

In October of the same year 'WPO-III' was superseded by still another plan – 'Rainbow V'. This was world-wide in scope and had been drawn up in consultation with the British General Staff. It was designed for a situation in which America was fighting both Japan and Germany. Germany was to be viewed as Enemy No 1, while the forces in the Philippines would adopt a defensive strategy similar to that of 'WPO-III'.

MacArthur disliked the negative and defensive approach of both these plans and wrote to Marshall in Washington suggesting that, with the growing forces at his disposal, the 'citadel-type defence' based on Bataan and Corregidor could be abandoned in favour of a plan aimed at keeping the

new command, to be known as United States Army Forces in the Far East (USAFFE). This was to be constitued in the Philippines to meet the growing threat of Japan and would combine the old Philippine Department and the forces of the Philippine Commonwealth into one integrated force. MacArthur accepted and the appointment became operative at the very moment that relations between Japan and America reached crisis-point.

For that July, following the Japansee occupation, with the connivance of the Vichy government, of French Indo-China, President F D Roosevelt had frozen Japanese assets in America. He thus cut off the supplies of Ameri-

Above: President Quezon greets General MacArthur, his new C-in-C. *Below left:* US Chief of Staff, General George Marshall. *Below right:* Major-General H Brereton, commander of the Far Eastern Air Force

Above left: Brigadier-General G M Parker, the South Luzon Force commander Above right: Admiral T C Hart, C-in-C Asiatic Fleet. Below left: Lieutenant-General R Sutherland. Below right: Major-General Wainwright

The Boeing B-17D Flying Fortress was generally similar to the earlier B-17C, but it was fitted with self-sealing fuel tanks and increased armour, which the service of the B-17C with the RAF had shown to be essential if the bomber were to survive against the increasingly heavy cannon and machine gun armament carried by all modern fighters. B-17Ds were built between February and September 1941, and thirty-five of these were in the Philippines when the Japanese attacked the islands.
Crew: eight to nine. *Engines:* four Wright R-1830-65 radials, 1,200hp each at 25,000 feet. *Armament:* six .5-inch and one .3-inch Browning machine guns

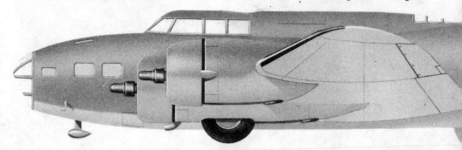

Japanese out of the Philippines altogether. Better still, if he could at the same time increase his air force to adequate strength, he believed he could pose a threat to Japan's sea-lanes southwards, blocking her movement of raw materials and disrupting her plans for conquest. To build up his forces for this task would take him about five months and he believed and hoped war would be delayed that long.

Marshall appeared enthusiastic and on 3rd November, Major-General Lewis H Brereton arrived in Manila to take command of a new air force, the Far Eastern Air Force (FEAF), which was to be built up in the islands on Mac-Arthur's suggested lines. Brereton – who had met MacArthur once before, while the airman was commanding the 13th Observation Squadron in France in 1918 – had brought with him Marshall's letter replying to MacArthur's request for a change of policy. This delighted the general so much that he jumped up from his desk, threw his arms round Brereton and said, 'Lewis, you are just as welcome as the flowers in May.' Turning to his Chief of Staff, Lieutenant-General Richard K Sutherland, he said, 'Dick, they're going to give us everything we've asked for.'

Shipments of men and supplies from the US at once increased, though they never reached the quantities Mac-Arthur wanted.

By the end of the first week of December ten divisions of the Philippine Army had been mobilised. They included 20,000 regulars and 100,000 totally raw Filipino reservists of the so-called Citizen National Army. Their state of training varied wildly from division to division and the call-up had been so ill-organised that some units were below strength while others were actually over-strength. Among this surplus were two batteries of artillery with a total of eighty guns; they remained idle until, with the rest of the excess, they were distributed among other units. Because of this mistake the training of artillery, an arm which was to prove vital, did not begin until after hostilities had started.

Many of the Filipino troops were illiterate and, on top of this, there were enormous language difficulties. Often, the men spoke nothing but their local dialect while their officers knew only English, Spanish or Tagalog, the tongue spoken in Manila and its environs. There was a shortage of light artillery and machine guns and the small arms were Enfield rifles of

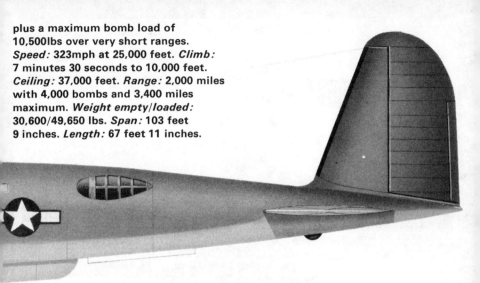

plus a maximum bomb load of 10,500lbs over very short ranges. *Speed:* 323mph at 25,000 feet. *Climb:* 7 minutes 30 seconds to 10,000 feet. *Ceiling:* 37,000 feet. *Range:* 2,000 miles with 4,000 bombs and 3,400 miles maximum. *Weight empty/loaded:* 30,600/49,650 lbs. *Span:* 103 feet 9 inches. *Length:* 67 feet 11 inches.

First World War design. Their uniforms consisted of shorts, a short-sleeved shirt – both totally unsuitable for the long cold nights to come – and a pair of canvas shoes which wore out in a couple of weeks. There were no replacements of uniforms or weapons and there were no steel helmets.

In most respects, they were a *levée-en-masse* rather than an army. The only units which showed any signs of discipline and cohesion belonged to the Philippine Scouts, a mixed American and Filipino force. Nominally the Scouts were part of the 10,473 strong Philippine Division, which also included the 31st Regiment, the only wholly American infantry unit in the islands. The division possessed some artillery including two batteries of British 75mm guns and a battery of 2.95-inch pack mountain guns.

In practice, the Philippine Division, without doubt the most reliable force in the islands, hardly ever operated as a separate unit, and was almost always split up.

Despite all these snags and imponderables MacArthur had, in numbers at least, a far stronger force than any of his predecessors and certainly a greater one than the US war-planners who drew up 'WPO-III' had envisaged.

Furthermore, from as far back as September, reinforcements had been reaching him. They included the 200th Coast Artillery Regiment (Anti-aircraft) with twelve 3-inch guns and twenty-five 75mm guns on self-propelled mounts which arrived in mid-October. He also received 108 M-3 light tanks and on 21st November a Provisional Tank Group was established under the command of Colonel James R N Weaver.

In terms of air strength, too, MacArthur was more fortunate than those who had gone before him, though in fact considering the magnitude and urgency of the threat, his force was growing too slowly.

In October nine Boeing B-17 'Flying Fortresses' had landed at Clark Field, Manila, followed by fifty fighters. Ultimately Brereton's operational strength was thirty-five 'Flying Fortresses' and seventy-two fighters, mostly Curtiss P-40 'Kittyhawks'. This was about a third of the number MacArthur had requested, but it was, all the same, a formidable force and his later claims that his air force was 'hardly more than a token force' do not stand up. Certainly in November 1941 General Marshall felt perfectly justified in telling a Press conference

NORTH LUZON FORCE
(Wainwright)

4 PHILIPPINE INF. DIVS.
1 US CAV. REGT.

RESERVE FORCE
(Moore)

1 PHILIPPINE INF. DIV.

SOUTH LUZON FORCE
(Parker)

2 PHILIPPINE INF. DIVS.
1 US BTRY. FIELD ARTILLERY

VISAYAN-MINDANAO FORCE (Sharp)

3 PHILIPPINE INF. DIVS.

Force sector boundary
0 Miles 200
0 Kilometres 300

LUZON

Manila

Batangas

Legaspi

MINDORO

MASBATE

SAMAR

VISAYAN SEA

PANAY

LEYTE

PALAWAN

NEGROS

CEBU

BOHOL

MINDANAO

Jolo I.

BORNEO

US command structure for the defence of the Philippines

that the position of the Philippines was now excellent. He spoke of the B-17s as the 'greatest concentration of heavy bomber strength anywhere in the world' and said they could counter attack and set the 'paper cities of Japan' ablaze, while at the same time making the Philippine garrison independent of sea-power.

With his strength thus growing and having gained approval for his plan to defend the islands in their entirety, MacArthur now began to organise his forces and make his dispositions. It was no easy task so to organise the defence of a group of more than 7,000 separate volcanic islands as to deny the enemy entrance. It was, however, one he had undertaken voluntarily.

The greatest land mass in the Philippines is Luzon, covering an area of nearly 41,000 square miles. It is largely mountainous with peaks rising to over 6,000 feet above sea level, the highest of them to nearly 10,000 feet. Dividing these mountain chains are two plains. The more northerly, stretching as a natural corridor between the mountains on either side of the Cagayan River, runs from the north coast to a point at which the two mountain chains join. The Central Plain, further south, runs from the Gulf of Lingayen, on the West coast, to Manila itself. MacArthur was to claim both at the time and subsequently that he had divined that the Japanese would land at Lingayen Gulf. This belief was based not only on logical deduction – its suitability for deploying large forces, its proximity to Manila and so on – but also on the predictions made by Homer Lea in his book, *The Valor of Ignorance*, published in 1911. Lea had correctly forecast the growth of Japanese aggression in Asia and suggested Lingayen as the most likely landing point for their forces to land in the Philippines. We shall see later how MacArthur responded to this twice-supported assessment of where the Japanese main blow was likely to fall.

Since Luzon was the biggest island the main defensive concentration would obviously have to be here. MacArthur divided his forces on Luzon into two groups. The larger, called the North Luzon force, was placed under Lieutenant-General Jonathan Wainwright. Wainwright came of a distinguished American military family with connections going back to the Civil War, but was himself a typical American professional soldier of the inter-war years. Graduating from West Point in 1906, the first thirty-four years of his career had been largely uneventful. His combat experience had been gained against the Philippine insurgents and as a staff officer in France in the First World War. In 1938 he was made a brigadier-general and two years later sent to Manila to command the Philippine Division then being formed. A tall, thin, rangy man whose experience lay mainly in cavalry, he was about to embark, as William Craig put it, in 'The Fall of Japan', 'upon the climactic assignment of his career – and perhaps the most cruel duty any American general endured during the entire war'.

For his latest mission MacArthur gave him four infantry divisions, including one of Philippine Scouts, as well as the 26th Cavalry, Philippine Scouts; two batteries of 155mm guns and one battery of 2.95-inch mountain guns. In addition, the 71st Division, Philippine Army, was assigned to him, though it could be committed only on the authority of USAFFE.

The smaller Luzon force, the South Luzon Force, was under Brigadier-General George M Parker, jnr, and was to cover the lower parts of the island from the Batangas to Legaspi – where attackers from the Japanese mandate Caroline Islands could be expected to land. The force consisted of two Philippine army divisions and a battery of field artillery.

The second biggest island is Mindanao, at the southern extremity of the archipelago, and covering an area of 36,906 square miles. This was placed

US officers inspect Filipino troops on Mindanao

under the command of Brigadier-General William F Sharp with two Philippine army divisions and a battery of artillery, while the group of small islands – jointly known as the Visayas – which link the two big ones and include Cebu, Leyte, Panay, Negros, Samar, Masbate and Bohol, was under the command of Brigadier-General Bradford G Chynoweth. The force there was made up of three Philippine army divisions.

While MacArthur was making his land dispositions his Naval counterpart, Admiral Thomas C Hart, commander of the Asiatic Fleet, was considering how he could best use what forces he had available. Hart, with forty-four years service behind him, had been in command of the Asiatic Fleet for just over two years. A slight man with a quick temper, he had earned himself a reputation for being

a strict disciplinarian. Nor was any love lost between him and MacArthur. Hart regarded the general as egotistical and histrionic. MacArthur looked on the admiral as a pessimist and a defeatist. On one occasion, shortly after the war began, he reported angrily to Marshall that Hart had refused to provide an escort to Manila for a convoy of guns, ammunition and aircraft which had been diverted to Brisbane, Australia. Hart, he declared, 'seemed to be of the opinion that the islands were ultimately doomed'. This complaint that the Navy lacked dynamism and aggressive spirit was one to which he frequently returned.

On his side, Hart believed that MacArthur was temperamentally incapable of seeing the obvious limitations of a fleet as tiny as his. It consisted of one heavy cruiser, the *Houston*, two light cruisers, thirteen First World War destroyers, twenty-eight submarines and a number of auxiliaries. Besides these he had at Olongapo, in

Subic Bay, the 4th Marines, an élite force of 750 men under Colonel Samuel L Howard, and his small Naval air force. This comprised twenty-eight 'Catalina' flyingboats – three of which were attached to the tender, *William B Preston*, four utility planes, and one observation plane. The whole force was organised as Patrol Wing 10.

In the autumn of the previous year he had transferred his units from China to Manila Bay. Under the existing plans his small fleet was responsible for the defence of the Philippines and for helping the army as much as it could, but Hart, like everyone else in the islands, had no delusions about what so small a force could do. He believed its best hope lay in a delaying action based on Manila Bay, while waiting – as under 'WPO-III' the land forces were to wait – for deliverance by the Pacific Fleet.

However, as early as 20th November he had been ordered by the Navy Department to leave Manila and move his ships southwards where it was believed they would be out of the reach of the Japanese. Except for the submarines, which were to be used to try to sink the invasion transports, and some of the Catalinas, needed for reconnaissance duties, his fleet had already gone. The only vessels now in the bay were four of his destroyers, six river gunboats and five minesweepers, as well as an assortment of auxiliaries.

On 27th November Hart had received warning from the Navy Department in Washington that an 'aggressive move by Japan' could be expected. Among likely places for this were Borneo, the Kra Peninsula – the narrow neck of land down which Thailand runs into Malaya, or the Philippines.

This information came from the top-secret diplomatic messages sent by the Japanese over their 'Magic' net-

Troop ship arrives in answer to MacArthur's request for reinforcements

work in a code which the Americans had succeeded in breaking down. Several of these messages had mentioned 29th November as a 'deadline date' and it was assumed that this was the day chosen by the Japanese for whatever they had in mind.

Both Hart and MacArthur acted on this warning. Hart increased patrol activity of his Catalinas and MacArthur ordered the B-17s, which were at Clark Field and other air bases near Manila, to be moved to places where they were less vulnerable to air attack. This, however, proved both a slower and more difficult move than it appeared because the only fields in the south which were beyond Japanese

range were expecting the arrival of more Flying Fortresses from Hawaii and space had to be left for them. Furthermore, in view of the new plans, the bombers might have to make a quick counterstrike after Japan declared war, and for this they needed to be in a place where they could be made ready. In the end only about seventeen were moved south.

Though the Japanese had mentioned the date of 29th November, they had been too cautious to specify the actual date and place of their intended moves. This meant that all American bases in the Philippines, as elsewhere, had been put on the alert, and, inevitably, when Saturday, 29th Nov-

ember and then Sunday, 30th, passed uneventfully, expectancy fell off.

Appreciating this and finding that intercepted Japanese codes still pointed to great activity accompanied by strong stress on secrecy, the Office of Naval Intelligence wanted to send out a second war warning on 4th December. This, however, was vetoed at higher level.

Nonetheless, on that day MacArthur ordered his interceptor aircraft to begin night patrols of territorial waters. Each night thereafter they came upon Japanese bomber groups twenty to fifty miles out to sea. Each time they turned away before reaching the International Line.

The most famous and successful flying-boat and amphibian of all time, the PBY-5A illustrated being the first amphibian version to be produced in quantity. *Engines:* two Pratt & Whitney R-1830-92 radials, 1,200hp each at take-off. *Armament:* two .5-inch and three .3-inch Browning machine guns, plus four 325-lb depth charges, or up to 4,000 lbs of bombs or two torpedoes. *Speed:* 178mph at 7,000 feet. *Climb:* 630 feet per minute initially. *Ceiling:* 16,200 feet. *Range:* 2,535 miles patrol, 1,405 miles with four depth charges, 2,195 miles with 2,000 lbs of bombs. *Weight empty/loaded:* k1,480/36,400 lbs. *Span:* 104 feet. *Length:* 63 feet.

Plans and Decisions

For the Japanese there were four barriers to their ambitions in the Pacific: the French in Indo-China; the British in Singapore – supported to a degree by the Dutch in the East Indies; the American Pacific Fleet; and lastly, the growing strength of the Far Eastern Air Force in the Philippines.

By the middle of 1940 France's defeat in Europe had removed her as a force to be reckoned with in the Pacific, while Britain, without the Pacific Fleet (which her naval strategists had been urging for twenty years as the only way to protect her Far Eastern possessions), was heavily committed near home. There remained only the costly Singapore base from which to make an empty gesture of Imperial might at the point of the Malay Peninsula.

The British Army, the Japanese knew, was represented by the Imperial III Corps, made up of no more than thirty-two infantry battalions or the equivalent of three weak and poorly armed divisions. These had been drawn mainly from Australia and India and had been given no special training, such as in jungle warfare, before taking their place in the line. In terms of air forces the British had 150 planes, all lacking in range (in a zone where range was essential), and in most cases out of date. Replacements could not be made because both the aircraft and ships which might have carried them were needed to help the Russian army to keep fighting.

In November 1941, as negotiation with America seemed to be moving towards deadlock, the Japanese Imperial General Staff began detailed war planning. The conquest of the Philippines was conceived of as part of the Great East Asia War which would also include the seizure of Malaya, Thailand, Borneo and the Dutch East Indies. On 6th November the Southern Army was created for this task with General Count Hisaichi Terauchi, a former war minister, as its commander. His forces comprised the Fourteenth, Fifteenth, Sixteenth and Twenty-first Armies, in all ten divisions and three mixed brigades.

The Fourteenth Army was assigned to the capture of the Philippines and Terauchi appointed Lieutenant-General Masaharu Homma its commander. Homma, then commander-in-chief in Formosa, had already held combat command in the China war. Built like a heavyweight boxer, an appearance enhanced by his clean shaven head, he was exceptionally tall for a Japanese – his height of five foot ten inches set him head and shoulders above most of his colleagues.

Outward appearances, however, concealed a shrewd, original and quick-thinking mind. He was now forty-seven and had behind him a wealth of experience. After graduating from the Japanese Military Staff College he had been sent, in the last year of the First World War, as Military Attaché to the Japanese Embassy in London, and then in 1922, to India. Later, as chief of the Army Press Bureau, he had learned better than most of his fellow-generals to understand the importance of good press relations, and Japanese war correspondents were usually in his entourage.

Plans for the taking of the Philippines had already been drawn up by the Imperial General Staff, and in mid-November Homma, together with the other commanders both Naval and military, was shown these at a series of meetings presided over by the Prime Minister, Tojo, who was also War Minister. It was explained to them how the strike on Pearl Harbor would remove the American Pacific Fleet, leaving 'as the only naval opposition Hart's small Asiatic Fleet.

The Japanese planners were not, however, leaving anything to chance and appointed Vice-Admiral Ibo Takahashi, Commander-in-Chief of the 3rd

Lieutenant-General Homma, entrusted with the Japanese conquest of the Philippines

Fleet, to be responsible for naval cover to the landings on the Philippines, giving him a powerful fleet for the task. At the same time Takahashi was to direct all naval and amphibious operations until Homma came ashore with the main invasion forces landing on Luzon. Takahashi divided his fleet into two forces with one at Formosa and the other at Palau in the Caroline Islands.

Final details were drawn up between Homma and his fellow-commanders at a conference at Iwakuni, in Southern Honshu, from 13/15th November. Here it was decided that because of the presence of the Far Eastern Air Force, an attack on the Philippines must fall into two distinct, mutually dependent phases. First there was to be a powerful air strike aimed at destroying the capability of the Far Eastern Air Force to attack Formosa or mainland Japan. In this way, America's war potential in the Pacific

both at sea and in the air – the two spheres which most counted in the region – would be obliterated. At the same time the way would be opened for the second phase of the operation which was to follow quickly. This would consist of seaborne landings on the main islands, aimed at their speedy neutralisation. The Japanese could then advance unmolested on their march of conquest through South-East Asia.

It is a measure of Japanese confidence (or arrogance) that the forces assigned to this task were comparatively small: two full divisions, the 16th and 48th, together with two tank regiments, two regiments and one battalion of medium artillery, three engineer regiments and five anti-aircraft battalions. With forces like this Homma was to take on the ten divisions available to the USAFEE. This confidence was the result not only of a conviction that their troops

The Misubishi Ki-30 Army Type 97 Light Bomber (codenammed ANN by the Allies) was a viceless but undistinguished light bomber while operating against the Chinese in the late 'Thirties, but when sent into action against the better fighters of the US in the Philippines in 1941-42, it proved to be easy meat for them. It was soon relegated to training duties. *Crew:* two. *Engine:* one Army Type 97 (Nakajima Ha-5 KAI) air-cooled radial, 950hp at take-off. *Armament:* two Type 89 7.7mm machine guns (one fixed and one flexible), plus up to 882 lbs of bombs. *Speed:* 263mph at 13,165 feet. *Climb:* 10 minutes 36 seconds to 16,405 feet. *Ceiling:* 28,120 feet. *Range:* 1,056 miles. *Weight empty/loaded:* 4,916/ 7,324 lbs. *Span:* 47 feet 8¾ inches. *Length:* 33 feet 11 inches.

General Count Terauchi, in command of the Southern Army

Vice-Admiral Tsukahara's 11th Air Fleet would cover the landings

were superior as fighting forces, but also of an exact knowledge of the defence situation.

For years the Japanese espionage system had been amassing details of the positions and sizes of the American bases in the Philippines, as well as of the suitability of the islands as a jumping off ground for a subsequent attack on Borneo and the Dutch East Indies which lay to the south. Ever since the middle 'thirties they had come in their thousands, through the port of Davao, at the southerly tip of Mindanao. They came as businessmen, itinerant photographers, or cycle salesmen and travelled through every town and hamlet. They helped their Imperial High Command to build up a picture of the situation in the islands and to be informed about Philippine life down to the smallest local details.

This bank of knowledge was to be of great use to the army later. More immediately, it enabled the air force strategists to draw up plans for the defeat of the Far Eastern Air Force, a step regarded as vital both to success in the Philippines and to that of the attack on Pearl Harbor. Knowledge of the damage that well organised espionage could do had, however, made them nervily-security conscious themselves. They were mainly concerned at this stage that the Americans might gain prior warning and move their aircraft from the main airfield complex round Manila to bases in the south where they would be beyond the range of the Japanese planes. Indeed, as we have seen, these moves were already beginning.

To avoid giving the Americans time to evacuate, the air strikes against their bases were scheduled to take place on 'X-Day', the first day of war, and as soon after the attack on Pearl Harbor began as possible. The original intention had been to make them coincide, but this had proved impossible as it was still dark in Formosa for some hours after sunrise in Hawaii. The attacks on the Philippines could not therefore take place until three

hours after the assault on the Pacific Fleet, at the earliest, but it was agreed that provided this timetable was closely adhered to, and the Japanese aircraft were not delayed longer than this, all should be well.

As a further precaution against discovery of their intentions the Japanese forbade aerial or submarine reconnaissance before the attack, with the exception of high altitude air photography of the places the army was later to invade.

Using the Intelligence sources on which so much patience and care had been expended, Lieutenant-Colonel Tokutaro Sato, operations chief of the Fourteenth Army, estimated that the Americans had some 200 combat-ready aircraft. (This was actually a liberal estimate as MacArthur's staff put it at about 150). Relying on these figures the Japanese assigned two air forces to the Philippines campaign. These were: the 5th Air Group of Army Air Force, commanded by Lieutenant-General Hideyoshi Obata, which was to provide 307 first-line aircraft, including Mitsubishi Ki-21 heavy bombers, as well as Kawasaki Ki-15 and Mitsubhishi Ki-30 light bombers, plus supporting elements; and the Navy's 11th Air Fleet, commanded by Vice-Admiral Nishizo Tsukahara which would supply 444 land- and carrier-based aircraft, mostly Mitsubishi Zero-Sen fighters ('Zeros') and Mitsubishi Type-1 twin engined bombers ('Bettys'), making an overall total of 751 aircraft. This was calculated to give them the three-to-one ratio they believed necessary to ensure supremacy over the Americans.

Among the difficulties facing the air planners was that of how the Japanese aircraft would reach targets which lay at the extremity of their range. Carrier-borne planes would have solved this problem, but only one small carrier, the *Ryujo*, could be spared from the Pearl Harbor strike force. It was agreed, therefore, by the army and navy air force commanders that the navy, whose planes had the longer

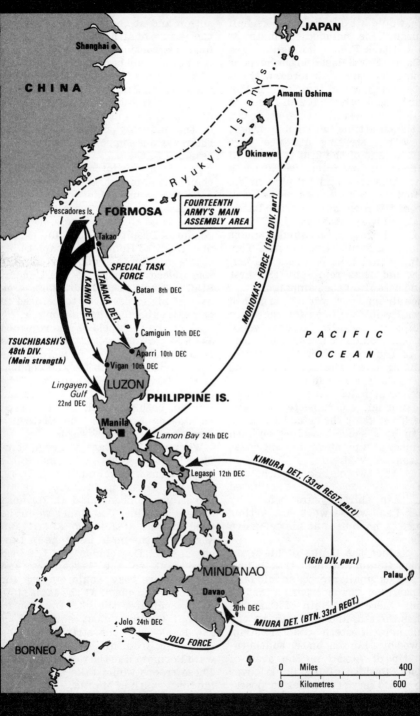

Japanese landings in the Philippines

range, would attack the southern half of Luzon. This included the main air base at Clark Field, the Manila area and Cavite Naval Base and the harbour defences. The army air force, with its shorter reach, would attack the half of Luzon lying north of a line drawn from the Gulf of Lingayen to the west coast.

At the same time, as airfields of their own within striking distance were essential, one of the first tasks of all advanced landing forces would be to secure American and Filipino fields. As a further preliminary a special task force of 500 men was to seize Batan Island, midway between the Philippines and Formosa, and quickly adapt the landing strip there for use. This landing would take place on 'X-Day' and would thus represent the first ground assault of the campaign.

Once air superiority had been gained the way would be open for the main amphibious assaults. These would take place on 22nd December in the Gulf of Lingayen. From here forces advancing down the corridor of the Central Plain would move on Manila where the principal set piece battle of the campaign was expected to take place. To envelop the defenders, there was to be a second landing on 24th December at a point on the east coast of Luzon, below Manila.

Thus, the two main axes of attack were exactly along the lines predicted more than thirty years before by Homer Lea, whose work MacArthur claimed to have used as his defensive textbook.

To protect the flanks of his main advance Homma decided that before they struck smaller forces should land at Aparri on the northern coast of Luzon, where the Plain of Cagayan reaches the sea, and at Vigan, on the small north-western coastal strip, followed by a landing on the southernmost tip of Luzon in the area of Legaspi. Besides giving flank cover these would serve two other purposes: they would, he hoped, divide and draw the defenders away in sufficient numbers to ease the way for the main

action and at the same time lead to the seizure of airfields from which the final destruction of the Far Eastern Air Force could be completed. Because of the limited forces available for the whole campaign it was necessary to be very parsimonious in allocating men for these subsidiary attacks and in the end only six battalions with their various support units could be assigned to them.

Once Homma's forces had completed their envelopment and crushed the defenders round Manila, the island fortresses of the bay were to be neutralized and then the whole of Luzon occupied. Despite his small forces, the plan required Homma to complete his entire mission in about fifty days. It was indeed essential to the General Staff's planning that he did, for a large part of his forces were to be used in campaigns beyond the Philippines.

Since the archipelago was regarded as an important stepping stone to the Dutch East Indies, plans were at the same time drawn up for the occupation of Davao in Mindanao and of the island of Jolo between Mindanauo and Borneo, both of which could be used as staging areas for the Sixteenth Army's advance southwards.

When all these plans had been completed Homma began to make his dispositions within Fourteenth Army. The 48th Division, including its air forces, was concentrated at Formosa and its airfields. The planes would be used for the attacks on Aparri and Vigan and the main landings in Lingayen Gulf. Detachments of the 48th were sent to the Pescadores and Palau where they would embark for landings at Legaspi. At the same time he concentrated the 16th Division in Amami Oshima, most northerly of the Ryukyus – the strip of islands stretching from mainland Japan toward Formosa like the tail of a dragon. These troops would take part in the landings south of Manila.

During the final concentration and loading period secrecy round the ports was such that only a handful of officers

Above: the Ryujo supplied the only carrier-based air support for the invasion. *Below:* Japanese fighters prepare to take off to destroy the American fleet at Pearl Harbor during Operation Z

on Homma's staff knew the complete plan. This select band had to travel constantly through the embarkation zones answering questions and solving difficulties as they cropped up. Even so there was enormous confusion. Unit commanders were given the briefest possible information and complicated orders were issued only just before they were to be executed, so that there was little time for critical evaluation. Any ensuing problems had to be solved on an *ad hoc* basis with the officers never sure that they were not, by their own well-intentioned efforts, sabotaging the whole operation.

During this period, in readiness for the air attacks, the 21st and 23rd Air Flotillas of Vice-Admiral Tsukahara's 11th Air Fleet were stationed at Formosa, with smaller detachments at Palau.

At the same time, as the attacking forces, amid such great secrecy, were manoeuvring into position, the American forces throughout the world were anxiously on the alert after the warning of 27th November. In the Philippines Hart was making what preparations he could and MacArthur had begun his interception flights, on consecutive nights encountering Japanese bomber formations.

What Hart and MacArthur did not then know was that at an Imperial Conference attended by Emperor Hirohito three days before – on 1st December – the decision to go to war had been taken.

At the same time, too, the fleet for 'Operation Z', the strike against Pearl Harbor, was already three-quarters of the way on its voyage across the Pacific.

'X-Day' had been set for the 7th December. It was on the evening of that day that three Japanese task forces set sail from Formosa under cover of darkness. Two were making for Northern Luzon and one for Bataan Island.

The attack on Pearl Harbor signalled the start of the Philippine invasion

The First Acts of War

Admiral Hart was not the sort of man you telephoned in the early hours of the morning without good reason. But Lieutenant-Colonel William T Clement, who was doing his turn as duty officer, knew, when he picked up the telephone in the Marsman Building, headquarters of the Asiatic Fleet, at three o'clock Manila time, on that morning of Monday 8th December 1941, that he had good reason.

'Admiral,' he said, 'put some cold water on your face. I'm coming over with a message.'

Hart's apartments were about 300 yards away from the Marsman Building in the Manila Hotel. One of the city's most modern hotels, it was home or haunt for most of the leaders of Philippine life, including the higher ranking American service officers and their families. With the threat of war, however, many of the wives and families had now been sent home and Clement, as he crossed the empty foyer and took the lift to Hart's floor, thought how lonely and desolate it now was.

In his room Hart sat on the edge of the bed and read the message Clement had brought: 'Air raid on Pearl Harbor. This is no drill.'

Clement explained how the radio operator in the Marsman Building had picked up the message from Hawaii and as the radio operator there happened to be a friend immediately recognised his 'fist' and so knew the alarm was genuine.

In Hawaii it would be 0800 on Sunday, 7th December, which meant that the Japanese had struck just after sunrise.

Hart picked up a pad and, in pencil, scrawled his first war dispatch to broadcast to his fleet: 'Japan started hostilities. Govern yourselves accordingly.' He had rehearsed the text over and over again in his mind during the past weeks, but when it actually came to writing it he found he was so nervous he misspelt it, writing 'yourseles' for 'yourselves'.

Then he dressed, ate a quick breakfast and at 0400 hours arrived at his office.

It was about half an hour earlier that MacArthur first heard the news. Significantly the information came not from Asiatic Fleet sources (Clement claimed later he had tried to telephone USAFFE headquarters but could get no reply and had told one of the staff duty officers at his home).

The man who told him was his chief of staff, Sutherland.

MacArthur, like Hart, lived in the Manila Hotel, occupying its penthouse with his wife, Jean (whom he had married four years earlier), his three-year-old son, Arthur, and their Cantonese nurse, Ah Cheu. They were one of the few families still in the hotel. MacArthur and his wife had discussed the question of whether she and the child should leave, but had come to the conclusion that by staying – particularly as he was a field-marshal in the Philippine Army – they would be showing their confidence in the Filipinos' ability to defend themselves.

Knowing the strength of the American forces in Hawaii, MacArthur's first reaction to the news was that, if the Japanese had indeed been so reckless as to attack there, they must have suffered a considerable beating. It was not until 0530 that he began unbelievingly, to learn of the disaster which had struck the Pacific Fleet.

The man who had first reported it to him, Sutherland, a touchy, unsmilingly competent man, was typically working late in the office when he heard it from a commercial radio

By one blow the Japanese navy now commanded the Pacific

station newscast. His response was equally typical. He reported to his commander, then informed all army commanders and ordered them to their battle stations.

It had been from the same commercial broadcast that Brereton, at Clark Field, the main base of the US Far Eastern Air Force, had heard of it, and had, in his turn, alerted his units.

Brereton was in many ways the antithesis of Sutherland. A professional flier, he gave the impression of being happier in the skies than when attending to administrative detail and of having little time for the desk-bound type of military executive of which Sutherland was the archetype. In fact his appointment to Manila that November had come as a pleasant surprise. When summoned to his superior to be told of it he had expected to receive a reprimand for negligence. That there should have been conflict between personalities as different as those of Sutherland and Brereton was to be expected. Before another twenty-four hours had elapsed, however, it was to have been

Above: Admiral Hart, Lieutenant-General Brett and Major-General Brereton
Below: A taste of what is to come; Japanese aircraft attack US shipping.

instrumental in bringing disaster.

Less than three hours after the three people so deeply involved had heard the news the first act of war against the Philippines occured. At dawn thirteen Japanese dive-bombers, accompanied by nine Zeros, attacked the *William B Preston* in the Gulf of Davao, off Mindanao. The attackers were thought to have come from the carrier *Ryujo*, one of the smallest in the Japanese fleet with a strength of thirty-six planes. One of the *Preston's* three Catalina flying boats was on patrol, but the other two were destroyed and a pilot killed. The *Preston* escaped without damage, however, and reached safe anchorage.

This attack was scarcely more than a preliminary encounter, a chance brush. In Formosa ground crews had worked through the night, under arc-lamps, arming and preparing the rows of aircraft for the real battle, in an atmosphere of heady expectation. They had no idea what was planned, but knew it to be of importance and

The first US target of the Japanese in the Philippines; USS William D Preston

were infected by the obvious tension of their superiors. At Fourteenth Army headquarters this tension was almost at breaking point. Homma and his staff knew that their success and that at Pearl Harbor were interdependent.

Then, at about the same time that Hart, MacArthur and Brereton heard it in the Philippines, news of the attack's success became general knowledge in Formosa. It was heard, however, with mixed feelings. Pilots, rising wearily from sleep, looked out to see the island engulfed in one of those impenetrable sea-fogs to which it is prone. The planes, except for those already on patrol, were grounded and if the fog continued the sacrifices and achievements of their compatriots in Hawaii, designed to make all the subsequent conquests possible, would be largely wasted. The Americans would

Left: Japanese aircrew prepare to bomb-up a Philippine-bound aircraft
Above: the Japanese arrive

quickly realise where the next blow was likely to fall, would disperse their Far Eastern Air Force out of reach, and take preventive measures.

Nevertheless, two squadrons managed to take off from Haito airfield, in Formosa, and struck the American bases at Baguio, the Philippine summer capital, and at Tuguegarao in Northern Luzon, causing considerable damage and heavy casualties. At dawn, too, the special task force landed unopposed on Batan Island, completely without the knowledge of USAFFE. Japanese air force troops went immediately to look at the island's Basco Airfield and found it barely suitable for fighters and in need of considerable enlargement if it was to be used for anything bigger. All the same, on the following day, the 24th and 5th Fighter Regiments began using the base, while a force was sent south from Batan

Island to Camiguin Island where a seaplane base was established thirty-five miles from the north coast of Luzon.

The landing at Batan and the preliminary raids could serve no purpose, however, unless the fliers waiting at Formosa on that first day of the war could get off the ground. But, at about 0900 the already jittery attackers had a new shock. Brereton, to avoid his B-17s being caught on the ground, had ordered them to take off on patrol without bomb loads. This order was monitored by the Japanese listening-stations and taken to mean that the Americans were on their way to attack Formosa. Gas-masks were distributed and as many planes as possible ordered aloft.

In fact, that order was just one strand in a net of misunderstandings, delays and disagreements, the details of which were never to be resolved. At 0500, Brereton had gone to USAFFE headquarters to request permission from MacArthur for a daylight bomb-

ing mission against Formosa. As MacArthur was not available Sutherland told Brereton to go ahead with arming his planes, but not to mount the attack until he had been given permission directly from MacArthur. Two hours later Brereton went back and was again told to stand fast for orders from the Commander-in-Chief.

Then, two things happened. Brereton's air force chief, General Henry Arnold, telephoned from Washington giving him details of the Pearl Harbor attack and warning him to get his planes in the air so as to avoid a repetition of what had happened there. At the same time reports began coming in of enemy aircraft in the vicinity.

It was this which had led Brereton to order his B-17s to take off on patrol. At 1000 Brereton renewed his request for the attack and again an answer was deferred. The truth of the matter was that there were doubts at USAFFE headquarters about the attack's feasibility. The pilots, it was said, lacked vital information ,and there had been

no photographic reconnaissances – though no one explained why this had not been carried out.

Brereton, therefore, ordered a photographic reconnaissance mission to Southern Formosa. As this instruction was being out into action, MacArthur – Brereton claims – telephoned and it was agreed the attack should take place that afternoon when the results of the mission had been evaluated.

At about 1130, six-and-a-half hours after his original request had been made, ground crews began arming Brereton's aircraft. At the same time the B-17s still on patrol were recalled and loaded with 100 and 300lb bombs while all patrolling interceptors were brought back to be refuelled. The pilots, expecting to take off early in the afternoon, went for an early lunch.

In Formosa, about the same time, the fog began to lift and, shortly after, 108 bombers, escorted by 84 fighters, took off. They left convinced it was too late, that the Americans would have moved their aircraft out of range.

There was only one radar set working in the Philippines, but, at about the time that the greater part of the American Far Eastern Air Force was on the ground being fuelled or armed at Clark, Nicholls and Iba Airfields, the approaching enemy aircraft were spotted. Simultaneously, an observation post in the north of Luzon gave warning of the force to the plotting room at Nielson Field and soon after watchers all down the Luzon coast were reporting the movement of a high-flying force travelling towards Manila. A warning was passed from Nielson to Clark Field by teleprinter. Another warning was broadcast over the forces radio network. The teleprinter message never arrived because, it was said later, the inexperianced operator had left his machine to go to lunch. The radio message was drowned by static probably caused by the Japanese themselves.

The only message which did get through was one telephoned by a senior officer at Nielson and taken by a junior officer at Clark, who promised to deliver it 'at the eariest opportunity'. Whatever the causes or explanations the fact remains that only one American pursuit squadron, the 3rd, at Iba got off the ground.

At 1215 the first waves of Japanese attackers, flying in V-formation, were over the airfields and saw to their delight that, despite all the opportunies and time they had been granted, the American aircraft were still on the ground. At Clark were two squadrons of B-17s filled with bombs and fuel for the raid on Formosa and with them were the P-40s of the 20th Pursuit Squadron. At Nicholls the 17th Pursuit Squadron, which was supposed to cover Clark Field, had just landed to refuel.

The Japanese began dropping their bombs from an altitude of 22,000 feet and then made off.

The defenders now awoke to what was happening. Men rushed to the anti-aircraft guns as a second V-formation of bombers appeared. The guns, however, had no up-to-date ammunition and their shells burst from 2,000 to 4,000 feet below the bombers, which attacked with impunity and no sense of urgency for fully fifteen minutes.

As the second wave of bombers flew off, thirty-four Zeros came in to deliver strafing attacks across the airfields. Then, just as the last twelve surviving aircraft of 3rd Pursuit Squadron, the only one to take to the air, were about to land, fifty-four Japanese planes struck at Iba field.

By the end of the day eighteen of the thirty-four B-17s had been destroyed and with them fifty-six fighters – or two-thirds of the force of interceptors – and twenty-six aircraft of various other types. Eighty men had been killed and 150 wounded and many of the air force installations and servicing sheds had been destroyed. The total cost to the Japanese had been seven fighters.

What had gone wrong? It has been suggested that the uncertainty about the attack on Formosa, which led to the B-17s being still on the ground when the Japanese struck, was due to the fact that MacArthur was under orders not to commit the first 'overt act of war'. The idea does not stand scrutiny. He knew that war had started. Not only had Pearl Harbor been attacked but so also had the Philippines themselves. It might be argued that he delayed the attack on Formosa because he wanted aerial reconnaissances made, but the evidence shows that the same order that prohibited him from committing the first act of war specifically permitted him to carry out any reconnaissances which might be needed in advance of hostilities.

MacArthur, for his part, claimed to have known nothing of any intended foray against Formosa until he saw it in a newspaper dispatch months later. Whether Brereton received, as he claimed, a telephone call from MacArthur authorising the aerial photography mission is still a matter of controversy. On the weight of evidence it seems unlikely that MacArthur was totally unaware of why the B-17s were on the ground when the Japanese attacked.

The following day another Formosan fog hampered Japanese activities, allowing the Americans to bury their dead and clear the debris. Nevertheless, that day Manila City had its first taste of air raids when, before sunrise, a squadron of Japanese planes flew over the city causing damage and casualties. It was the first of a series of raids which were to go on almost daily from now on.

A fresh body blow fell the next day, 10th December. The Army interceptor headquarters received warning that a force of enemy planes was approaching North Luzon. The force was made up of fifty-two bombers, which had been given an escort of a hundred Zeros as it was expected to encounter opposi-

tion from American carrier-based aircraft – of which in fact there was none. The attackers had come from the Japanese navy's shore bases and from the carrier *Ryujo*.

Against such a force the twenty P-40s and seventeen P-35 'Republics' which had been scrambled had no chance. Over North Manila the raiders split and one section struck at O'Neill and Nicholls Airfields and at Camp Murphy. The other, made up of about twenty-seven Bettys, flew over the Navy Yard at Cavite at an altitude which, like that of the planes attacking Clark two days before, put them out of range of the obsolete anti-aircraft shells.

For two hours the bombers flew back and forth, unhurriedly picking out targets and bombing them with great accuracy. Standing on the roof of the Marsman Building, Hart and a group of his fellow officers watched in helpless wrath the remorseless destruction of the base. By the time the bombers had passed, not only the yards but almost the whole city of Cavite was burning.

The repair shops and warehouses, the radio station, the sick-bay, the Marine barracks, the electricity power station and the whole of the Navy's reserve stock of some 200 torpedoes, needed in its efforts to repel any invasion fleets, were all destroyed. Ships lost included the minelayer *Bittern* and the submarine *Sealion*.

A wind, constantly changing direction, kept the flames fanned so that the task of the over-stretched fire fighters became impossible and in the end the yard had to be left to burn itself out.

There were two pieces of good fortune: that the bombers did not hit the Navy's heavily stocked ammunition stores; and that a fleet of forty merchant ships anchored in the bay also escaped damage and was able to sail. But it was small compensation for the entire loss of the great navy yard at Cavite.

Late that night all survivors were

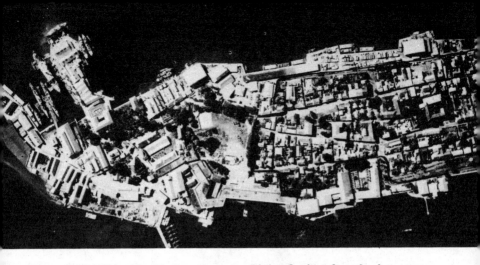

Above: Cavite Navy Yard before the war. *Right:* Cavite after the Japanese attack on 10th December

Above: USS Bittern and Below USS Sealion; both sunk at Cavite

assembled in a school playground nearby. The attack had caused some 500 casualties, who included not only navy personnel, but also Filipino civilians. Early the next morning Rear-Admiral Francis Rockwell of Hart's staff, his face blackened and his uniform bloodstained from helping the wounded, inspected the yard. He reported that all fires were completely out of control. A hasty salvage operation was started, a hospital was set up and ammunition and other supplies were moved out and dispersed in the Corregidor and Mariveles Naval bases.

There now came, however, a fresh disaster to the rapidly diminishing American air forces. By 12th December, the movement of the B-17s to the south had been almost completed, and reconnaissance aircraft, of which only about half remained, were to follow as soon as possible. Then, that morning, there came a report that a Japanese carrier fleet was moving upon Luzon and seven planes from the Navy's Patrol Wing 10 at Olongapo went out on a fruitless search.

Only when they were practically out of fuel did the planes return. As the tired crews came in to land, after days spent combing of the empty ocean, the Zeros which had been shadowing them struck. All seven – representing a quarter of the Asiatic Fleet's total of flying boats – were destroyed.

By the end of the fifth day of war a combination of the United States Far Eastern Air Force, the Filipino Air Force and the Naval Air Force had yielded the sky over the Philippines to the enemy. To defend the main island of the archipelago and its capital city, Brereton had only thirty-five operational fighters left and these were to be husbanded by being used mainly for reconnaissance rather than combat duties.

Hart had always had it in mind, once the first battles were over, to bring his ships, now in the south, back to Luzon, where they could provide a deterrent to amphibious landings. With no shore based aircraft to cover them, however, his ships would now stand no chance in trying to repel an invasion.

Nor was the gloom relieved by consideration of events elsewhere. With the Pacific Fleet destroyed, and the Asiatic Fleet immobilised, the only opposition on the high seas to Japan's aggression could come from the small Royal Netherlands Navy contingent based on the Dutch East Indies and the British Royal Navy.

Unable to defend her possessions in the Far East with her already fully extended naval forces, Britain had, instead, placed her whole reliance on the deterrent power of the American Pacific Fleet. When war with Japan appeared to be inevitable and Britain joined America in its embargoes on Japanese trade, it was obvious that these economic moves would have to be backed up by military forces to deny the Japanese the raw materials they needed, and which they would otherwise take for themselves. Churchill, activated not only by strategic but also by political considerations, overrode the protests of the First Sea Lord, Admiral Sir Dudley Pound, and proposed that the newly commissioned *Prince of Wales* and the battle-cruiser *Repulse* should be sent to the Pacific, with a fleet carrier to give air cover.

The two capital ships were duly sent, but an accident to the only aircraft-carrier available prevented it from sailing with them, so that they were left as wide open targets to Japanese air attack. On 10th December the Japanese took advantage of this situation. The two ships were spotted at 1100 hours. Two hours and twenty minutes later both had been sunk by torpedo-bombers. Destroyers rescued some 2,000 of the two ships' crews, but nearly 1,000 were drowned, including the Commander-in-Chief, Admiral Sir Tom Phillips and his Flag-Captain, John Leach. Both men had been in the Philippines only a few days before, discussing joint strategy with Hart and MacArthur.

Landings Begin

Such was the effect of the loss of the air forces and the destruction of the Cavite Navy Yard that the opening of the Japanese ground offensive on 10th December seemed unimportant by comparison.

The two initial landings had taken place as planned at Aparri and Vigan. Aparri is a port of 26,000 people situated at the mouth of the Cagayan river and at the head of the Cagayan valley. It can be reached from the Central Plain, where Manila stands, only by one pass through the mountains or by sea round the northern coast of Luzon. Vigan, which is the capital of Ilocos Sur Province, lies near the mouth of the Abra River about 250 miles from Manila, which is reached by a highway, Route 3. To the east of it lies the Cordillera range of mountains separating the narrow coast plain and the Cagayan valley.

Troops of the Apparri task force, 2,000 men from the 48th Division's 2nd Formosa Regiment, known after its commander, Colonel Toru Tanaka, as the Tanaka Detachment, had been one of three task forces which sailed from Formosa on the night of 7th December. The Vigan force, also drawn from the

Formosa Regiment and numbering 2,000 men, was the Kanno Detachment, named after the commander of the 3rd Battalion, 2nd Formosa. It had left at the same time. A naval cover force commanded by Vice-Admiral Takahashi included the two heavy cruisers *Ashigara* and *Maya*, two destroyers and a seaplane tender all of which sailed on 8th December.

The departure of these groups had been watched by General Homma and his staff with feelings of considerable apprehension. These advanced landings were essential to the success of the main thrust, and though, as advanced groups, the convoy had been given the fastest available ships, capable of twelve to fourteen knots, it seemed inconceivable they could escape detection by the Americans as they made the three-day crossing of the Philippine Sea. From daylight on the 8th, once the Formosan fogs had lifted, they were given cover by the 24th and 50th Fighter Regiments and throughout the crossing they were escorted by planes of the 5th Air Group.

In the early hours of 10th December they reached their anchorages. They had not seen a single US aircraft throughout the crossing.

By the early dawn light men of the Tanaka Detachment began transferring from the transport ships to the Daihatsu 'A' landing barges. These forty-nine foot long vessels, armed with two .25 calibre machine-guns and capable of a speeds of between eight

Japanese assault troops approach the Philippine beaches

and ten knots, each took 120 men.

The first two companies came ashore without opposition; not surprisingly, for the defence of the whole area north of Lingayen Gulf had been entrusted to the 11th Division, Philippine Army. The division, which had only begun to mobilise two months earlier was still a third below strength in its infantry regiments. It had no artillery, no transportation and its service elements had not yet been trained. Having to cover so large an area they had only been able to spare one battalion for the defence of the whole of the Cagayan valley.

But if military opposition was absent, the weather was providing Tanaka with difficulties of its own. a strong north-east wind was blowing and the breakers it had whipped up were causing heavy surf and making transfer from the transports to landing barges hazardous and the journey to the beaches uncomfortable and risky. Because of this, after the second company had reached shore, the convoy commander decided that the transports would have to be moved. They were then taken twenty miles eastward to Gonzaga where they were partially protected under the lea of Cape Engaño.

Late in the afternoon, when landing at the new site recommenced, the first reports reaching MacArthur's headquarters had resulted in two squadrons of P-40s and B-17s being sent into the attack. They hit a minesweeper which, after its depth charges exploded, became a total wreck. The violence of the attack was such that landing operations were once more held up.

The naval escort force, which was to cover all subsequent landings, was not eager to see its forces seriously weakened in their first brush with the

Japanese forces land unopposed at Aparri, Northern Luzon

enemy and wanted to retire quickly. They urged the transport crews to hurry, until in the end they were obliged to throw drums of oil overboard in the hope they would float ashore. Some heavy equipment, such as rollers which were needed for the air strips, could not be unloaded at all.

Despite these difficulties the whole of the Tanaka Detachment finally reached the shore unopposed. At Aparri a young American officer commanding a company of the 3rd Battalion, 12th Infantry, was ordered to attack immediately and drive the enemy into the sea. He estimated the two companies of the Tanaka Detachment at several times their actual strength and promptly withdrew south wards without firing a shot.

Just after midday the detachment was in possession of Aparri landing

Japanese marines secure the beachhead after the main landings on Lingayen Gulf

Japanese forces in the north move forward to protect the Lingayen landings

strip. When the airfield engineers who had landed with them saw it, however, they declared both it and another nearby as unfit for use by the heavy bombers. Thus one of the main purposes of the Aparri attack – that of providing airstrips from which the Americans could be brought under ceaseless bombardment – had been pointless. But so well were the air forces doing their work further south that the need for such fields no longer existed.

Meanwhile, at Vigan, the Kanno Detachment were experiencing the same sort of difficulties as their comrades at Aparri. Heavy seas prevented any of the detachment from landing and they had had to move four miles south under fighter cover. Here, at a more protected point, the 2,000 men of the detachment were landed. They were spotted, however, by a patrolling

Top: US submarine S 39. *Second, Third and Bottom:* the Japanese heavy cruisers Nachi, Myoko and Haguro which covered the main assault

Kittyhawk, at 0513. Five B-17s and a squadron of P-35s joined the attack. As at Aparri, bad weather was interfering with landing schedules. The small groups which did get ashore moved quickly to seize Vigan at 1030, but in the meantime air strikes had begun. Despite the anti-aircraft fire, low-flying bombers and fighters made desperate attacks. On one such run a Japanese transport hit by a bomb from a B-17 exploded with such force that it destroyed the squadron commander's plane.

The air attacks continued all day and represented the most spirited opposition to their landing the Japanese had yet met with in the Philippines. As a result they lost two of their *Maru* transports.

They were, none the less, the last coordinated efforts of the US Far Eastern Air Force. Further attacks on Nicholls, Nielson and Cavite Airfields had completed the destruction begun earlier and from now on aircraft were able only to fly patrols. And that day the Americans were forced to bemoan yet again the loss of their air force, for with very few more planes the invaders could have been turned back altogether at both Aparri and Vigan.

As it was the Tanaka Detachment, now safely established ashore, decided to reverse its former policy of caution, and pushed forward down the Cagayan valley.

When Wainwright, commander of the North Luzon Force, first heard of the landings, at that time estimated to be at the strength of a reinforced brigade (it was actually, of course, two battalions), he decided they were a feint and held his forces. The only path out of the valley was through the single mountain pass at Abalete. Here, he believed, it would require only a small force to stop a much greater one. All the same, he sent several scout cars of the 26th Cavalry, Philippine Scouts, up the Cagayan valley to establish communications with the Philippine 11th Division's troops in that area.

MacArthur's headquarters had, at the same time, ordered all bridges in the valley to be destroyed and a road block installed in the mountain pass.

The Tanaka Detachment was now moving southwards towards Tuguegarao along Route 5, while ahead of them army air force planes were bombing and strafing likely looking targets. Faced by this advance the 3rd Battalion, 12th Infantry, which had already avoided encounter with the enemy, retreated quickly down the Cagayan valley, offering no resistance, and fearful that it might be cut off. By 0530 on 12th December the Tanaka Detachment had taken its third airfield – that at Tuguegarao, more than fifty miles inside Philippine territory.

At the same time the Kanno Detachment, also now well-established ashore, sent a small force northwards and before evening occupied the capital of Ilocos Norte Province, Laoag, with its adjacent airfield. Both detachments, therefore, had three airfields in their possession.

USAFFE recognised the Tanaka and Kanno landings for what they were – the preliminaries to a major assault elsewhere – and realised that the main force had still to arrive. But the fear of fresh landings produced an invasion-fever, and during that night the men of one Philippine unit so far convinced themselves that the Japanese were attempting to land at Lingayen Gulf that they fought a noisy pitched battle with their imaginary foe. And the next day, despite the absence of any sign that the Japanese had come ashore, MacArthur's communiqué reported: 'An enemy landing was attempted in the Lingayen area, but was repulsed by a Philippine Army Division.'

It was later found that all the Japanese had done was to send a motor boat into the bay on a reconnaissance mission.

To Homma, in the meantime, it had become obvious that the Americans were not going to counterattack as he

had thought inevitable. He accordingly left only small forces guarding the newly captured airfields and, re-grouping the two landing detachments as one unit, sent them southwards towards Lingayen to meet the main invasion force when it came ashore. Colonel Tanaka was placed in charge of both detachments for this new mission and the two forces met on 20th December and at once began their advance out of Vigan, along Route 5 towards Lingayen.

The next day their advanced detachments encountered troops of the Philippine 11th Division, but in the battle that followed they outflanked the Filipinos by an eastward movement which pushed one section back and cut off the other. Tanaka then continued his advance and reached San Fernando, La Union, on the 22nd December – the very day on which the big blow was to fall. And so, right at the critical moment, he was ideally placed for an outflanking movement on any forces sent to hold the invaders.

As the Tanaka and Kanno Detachments were setting sail from Formosa still another was sailing from Palau in the Caroline Islands. They were to make for Legaspi at the southern extremity of Luzon where it narrows, like the tail of a stingray, into a strip of land.

The purpose of the landing was to acquire an airfield in the south and, at the same time, by gaining control of the San Bernardino Strait – the shallow channel which divides Luzon from the smaller Samar island – to stop the Americans from sending reinforcements through this route. To assist this operation two minelayers were sent with the invasion forces to lay minefields in all approaches.

For the landing 2,500 men from the 16th Division under Major-General Naoki Kimura were to be used. The force was made up of the 33rd Infantry

General A M Jones

Regiment, a battery of 22nd Field Artillery as well as additional engineer detachments and 575 men of the Navy's Kure 1st Special Landing Force. These last were naval units, somewhat like Marines, specially trained for seizing beaches.

The naval forces covering the landing were commanded by Rear-Admiral Takeo Takagi and had sailed from Palau on 6th December. They included the three heavy cruisers *Nachi*, *Haguro* and *Myoko*, a light cruiser, seven destroyers and two minelayers. Additionally, there was the aircraft carrier *Ryujo* whose planes were to provide air cover for the force and for the landings. It was these planes which in the early hours of the war had attacked the *William B Preston* and destroyed its aircraft.

On 9th December the troop transports caught up with Takagi's naval force and from a point about 100 miles off shore the *Ryujo's* planes began to provide air cover.

The journey was uneventful except for one encounter with an American submarine, the *S39*, which was driven off by a depth charge attack. As the convoy approached the beaches the naval escort remained behind to provide distant cover and aircraft from the carrier began offensive activity against the Legaspi area.

Filipino engineers prepare to blow a bridge to slow the Japanese advance from Legaspi

57

Shortly after this the 34rd Infantry and other army units began putting ashore, with none of the difficulties that the forces landing in the north had experienced, and without encountering opposition. The truth was that the nearest American troops were 150 miles away.

The first knowledge that USAFFE had of the landings came from the stationmaster at Legaspi who happened to be talking to USAFFE headquarters in Manila at the very moment they were taking place. Over the line he described them to the point at which a Japanese officer and a group of men walked into his office. The conversation is said to have ended when the Japanese asked for a train to take them to Manila and the stationmaster asked USAFFE what he should do. He was told: 'Tell them the next train leaves a week from Sunday.'

When the South Luzon Force was told of the landing, its first inclination was to consider bringing a strong force out to meet the Japanese and push them back into the sea. The plan was abandoned because it was felt the Filipino forces would be incapable of making the quick movements necessary for such an enterprise.

The Filipino forces responsible for the defence of the southern part of Luzon with its five sheltered bays and 250 miles of beaches, any of which could have been used for landing purposes, consisted of two divisions: the 41st and 51st. Both were poorly equipped and few of the infantry regiments had completed their training, while one had had no training at all. In view of this the only action that could be taken was to order the 51st Division, commanded by Brigadier-General Albert M Jones, to go south and destroy all possible road and rail bridges and evacuate as much railway rolling stock as possible.

It was another two days before, on 14th December, USAFFE managed to scrape together five very weary B-17s and sent them to attack the ships outside Legaspi. They went, but op-

position from Japanese naval pursuit planes was so heavy that only one aircraft returned to its base at Del Monte in Mindanao, the rest having to make forced landings where they could.

Three days later, on 17th December, the last of the Flying Fortresses left the Philippines altogether for Darwin, Australia. There was only one more sortie for them in Luzon.

On that same day, five days after their Legaspi landings, the Japanese encountered the first ground resistance, when a patrol ran into one of General Jones' demolition detachments. The Filipinos completed their job of destroying a bridge and then made off, leaving the Japanese to continue their advance.

They were not going much further unhindered, however. Towards the northern end of the Bicol peninsula

along which they were advancing, the land shrinks to a neck which at one point is a mere seven miles wide. Here Jones had outposted two companies from the 1st Battalion, 52nd Infantry, knowing that the Japanese must run into one or other. The encounter occurred on 22nd December when the Japanese struck Company B and suffered such heavy casualties they turned and ran, to be chased by the jubilant Filipinos for some six miles. The victory was small enough and it was to prove transient. It was, all the same, the sole success with which the South Luzon Force could console itself.

In the meantime there had been action further south. Two days before, on 20th December, the Japanese had landed a force of some 5,000 men at Davao, in Mindanao.

This force had sailed from Palau on

Despite delaying tactics by the Americans the Japanese advance

17th December under escort of a cruiser, six destroyers and auxiliary craft and aircraft from the *Ryujo* and the seaplane-carriers, *Chitose* and *Mizuho*. The only opposition the invaders met was from a Filipino machine-gun detachment which inflicted heavy losses until it was itself destroyed by a shell from one of the Japanese destroyers.

Although these landings were not intended to affect the Japanese effort further north and were only made to provide advance bases for the Sixteenth Army in its drive through southern Asia, they were, nevertheless, a means of isolating the archipelago from Allied bases in the south and so make more difficult the task of supplying the islands.

Transports off Lingayen

During the days before Christmas that year there was little feeling of festivity. In the churches of Manila with their strange mixture of Spanish baroque, Filipino, and Chinese architectural styles, the priests laid out the cribs for the *Fiesta de la Natividad* as they had done every year since the conversion of the island by the Augustinians in the 16th Century. There were few people to admire them, and the ecclesiastical authorities had stopped the *Misa de Gallo*, the series of nine early morning masses which lead up to the triumphant midnight mass of Christmas Eve, or *Buena Noche*. The

early morning was a favourite time for the Japanese raiders.

Manila, capital of the Philippines since the *conquistador*, Miguel Legazpi, had proclaimed it a province of Spain in 1571, was in normal times a bustling, cosmopolitan city of two million souls. They were now subjected to almost daily terror-raids. Those who could do so had left and those who could not leave had, in many cases, sent their families away.

Like most large Oriental cities it was densely populated with a concentration of 80,000 people per square mile and large areas of tenements and slums. The Japanese knew, therefore, that their raids could not fail to wreek enormous havoc. Some show of defence against the high flying bombers was made by the American and Filipino anti-aircraft gunners, but it was only occasionally that a pilot, more reckless or more daring than his comrades, came low enough to be reached. Then the local population – Chinese, Filipino, European – would be cheered by the sight of a blazing enemy plane crashing.

Yet somehow life went on. The shops and stores did business. The theatres and cinemas, usually showing Ameri-

can films, remained open. The smart, middle class Filipinio women haggled with the Chinese shopkeepers. People from the outlying villages brought their produce to market and presented a colourful enough scene: the women in their flowing 'Maria Clara' skirts, black with broad white stripes, the men in 'Barong Tagalog' shirts, with their heavy embroidery.

The Manila Symphony Orchestra gave concerts and the radio stations somehow kept on broadcasting jangling, wailing oriental music, the latest American jazz, or tense, chattering, defiant and often bombastic news bulletins. As far as possible, work went on normally in the business and government offices, great functional concrete blocks which the Filipino architects of the 'twenties, abandoning their own traditions, had aped from America as the symbol of success, modernity and wealth.

Morale, the government spokesmen declared in the newspapers, had never been higher. But the government spokesmen knew normality was only a thin crust all too often shattered as the bombers came again and the street emptied. They also knew that morale was daily weakening as the people realised more and more their helplessness before the Japanese onslaught.

Among those directly concerned was the mayor, Jorge Vargas, who had already made his views known to President Quezon. Quezon had appealed to MacArthur for American help to ameliorate the situation of the civil population and MacArthur, realising that the purpose of raids was to reduce the Filipinos to the point at which their sole concern would be to get rid of the *Yanquis* who had brought these troubles upon them, immediately applied to Washington. He was directly authorised by President Roosevelt to make available twenty million pesos for aid. This was to include the

The Japanese drive for Manila gets under way

Jorge B Vargas

housing of the homeless and the building up of some sort of air raid precaution system.

Then, three days before Christmas, the newspapers carried stories of new Japanese landings, this time in the Gulf of Lingayen. They reported American and Filipino troops resisting heroically to try to deny the enemy a foothold.

But at USAFFE headquarters the ominous truth was emerging. There it had already been recognised that these new landings represented the main Japanese effort for which they had been waiting. It was also realised that heroic resistance from the defence was the least of the Japanese problems. MacArthur was being forced to come to terms with the bitter truth that the Citizen National Army he had been organising and training for the past six years, and in which he believed so profoundly, was incapable of giving more than an impersonation of resistance.

A force of seventy-six army and nine naval transports now stood off Lingayen Gulf, carrying the main strength of the Japanese Fourteenth Army, as well as mountain and field artillery and about 100 tanks. These were mostly Shiki 94s, a medium tank of ungainly shape and high silhouette, first built in 1934, and armed with 37mm guns. They represented the first armour to be used by the Japanese in the Philippines and despite their – by Western standards – obsolete form, were to prove adequate to their role.

The ground forces were accompanied by a strong naval escort provided by the 3rd Fleet and under the personal direction of its commander, Admiral Takahashi. This task force had sailed in three separate convoys, each under its own escort, and if secrecy had attended the sailing of all the previous Japanese assault convoys it was redoubled in the case of those bound for Lingayen. Only a few people were allowed to know the destination and once troops were aboard the transports a ban on the use of maps added to their nervousness. This anxiety was shared by Homma and his staff, who were sailing with the convoys. They knew full well that all that had gone before was only preparation. As Homma said later, before the War Crimes Tribunal: 'During all my campaigns in the Philippines I had three critical moments. This was No 1.'

The first convoy had left Kirun in Formosa on 17th December and contained twenty-one transports; the second, from Mako in the Pescadores followed at noon on 18th; and the third, from Takao, Formosa, on the evening of the same day.

Besides their actual accompanying naval cover there were altogether two light cruisers, sixteen destroyers, and a large number of motor torpedo boats, minelayers and patrol craft backing the expedition, while units of Vice-Admiral Nabutake Kondo's 2nd Fleet, which had covered the Malayan landings earlier, were to give distinct cover.

The main ground combat force was Lieutenant-General Yuichi Tsuchibashi's 49th Division. This was composed largely of the 1st and 2nd Formosa Regiments, with the 47th Infantry Regiment, artillery, reconnaissance, engineer and transport units and other services units.

Fourteenth Army headquarters were, among their other concerns, worried about the Formosa Regiments These were untried in battle and the 2nd Formosa had already been reduced to provide the Kanno and Tanaka Detachments used in the Aparri and Vigan landings.

Under the attack plan, each convoy represented a separate task force and each was to land at a different point along the gulf. First ashore would be the men of the 47th Infantry and a detachment of the tanks. They would land at Agoo, the southernmost of the three points, five miles from the town of Damortis.

Thirty minutes later men of the 1st Formosa and a second tank unit would begin landing at Caba, seven miles north of Agoo. The third force, called the Kamajima Detachment, would start landing about half an hour later still, at Bauang, seven miles north of Caba. If all went well the Fourteenth Army would have established a bridgehead fifteen miles long stretching from Bauang to Agoo by the early morning of D-Day.

To land this force the Japanese had assembled nearly 200 landing craft. Sixty-three were the normal *Daihatsu* landing barges, seventy-three were larger ones, and fifteen were extra large craft called *Tokubestu Daihatsu*, while there even some forty-eight powered sampans.

The position chosen was an admirable one on the narrow coastal belt between sea and mountains. Along this strip ran Route 3, one of the main highways of Luzon, which had a junction at Bauang where a second road led through the mountain pass to Baguio. The area was also a concentration point for many roads into Manila, including Route 3 itself which south of the landing beaches ran through the wide Central Plain.

Once ashore, the assault troops were to liquidate opposition as quickly as

TANAKA & KANNO
DETACHMENTS

San Fernando

C o r d i l l e r a

C e n t r a l

KAMAJIMA DET.

Bauang   Naguilian

1st FORMOSA REGT.
+ TANK DET.

Santiago

3

Baguio 24th DEC.

47th INF. REGT.
+ TANK DET.

Caba

Agoo

L i n g a y e n

Rosario 22nd DEC

G u l f

Damortis

Sison

Lingayen   Dagupan

Binalonan
24th DEC

26th CAV. (PS.)

21st DIV.

Tayug

Urdaneta

71st DIV.

11th DIV.

91st DIV.

Aguila   San Carlos

Agno   Rosales

Z a m b a l e s

Carmen

M t s

3

13

C e n t r a l   *P l a i n*

Japanese landings and attacks 22/24th December

US positions (approximate) on night 24/25th December

| 0 | Miles | 10 | | 20 |
| 0 | Kilometres | 20 | | 40 |

Homma's main assault is launched against Lingayen Gulf

Above: Japanese tanks and infantry advance through Tayabas. *Right:* a Filipino unit prepares to resist the victorious Japanese

possible and move inland without waiting to consolidate. This task would fall to subsequent waves. The Kamajima Detachment was to split upon landing: one element would go northward to join up with Colonel Tanaka's Aparri force now moving southward with the Kanno Detachment; the other body would seize Naguilan Airfield, then advance to take Baguio. In this way the rear of the Japanese advance would be protected while the seizure of Baguio would prevent an American counter-attack from the east through the mountains.

The other two landing forces would move south to seize Damortis and Rosario, then re-form to advance southward.

The secrecy which had attended the

loading of the convoys did not cease once they had sailed. To confuse any chance observers of their movement the transports first travelled south westward as though en route for Indo-China, before turning toward their true destination. In the event such subterfuges were quite unnecessary. No American ships or planes appeared while the convoy was at sea, a fact which seemed to those aboard little short of miraculous and as yet further confirmation of the fact the war-gods of Japan were on their side. The only hazard they encountered, indeed, was a natural one: a typhoon in the South China Sea.

The Japanese were so convinced of their own air supremacy that the convoy was given no air cover until 21st December when twenty planes from the 24th and 50th Fighter Regiments, now able to fly from bases on Luzon itself, went out to meet the invaders.

That night, in cold, wet weather, under a darkening sky, the transports began dropping anchor in Lingayen Gulf. Everything had so far gone without a hitch, but from this point things began to go wrong.

The convoy leaders had been warned not to stop short of their targets, but, unable to find them in the darkness, they went to the other extreme and overshot, leaving the landing craft to make an extra long journey, throughout which they would be vulnerable to artillery.

Because of high seas it proved difficult to load the landing craft. Nevertheless, the landing operations were begun almost on schedule with the first troops touching down on Agoo beach at 0517. At 0530 the 1st Formosa Regiment and the main strength of the 3rd Battalion, 48th Mountain Artillery Regiment had landed. Two hours later the Kamajima Detachment started assembling on the beach at Bauang, while the rest of the detachment landed at Santiago, three miles to the south.

But the men had been soaked by

heavy spray. Signals equipment had been ruined by salt water – so that Homma, whose headquarters were aboard one of the ships, had no idea what was happening – while weather conditions were also making ship-to-ship communication difficult.

In the end the Bauang convoy was forced to weigh anchor and seek shelter near San Fernando. The second, consolidating, wave was unable to land at all. Heavy equipment could not be brought ashore, though during the day some infantry, mountain artillery and armour was unloaded.

Only the seamanship of the transport commanders saved the landings from disaster. They navigated their vessels into the shallows, though they still had them spread out in a line some fifteen miles long, an open target if there had been the forces available to take advantage of the fact.

Meanwhile, Homma, cut off from information about what was happening to his troops, knew that, after the confusion caused by the high seas, should they encounter determined and well-planned resistance, they must be pushed back. He was in a dither of nerves.

Opposition, however, was negligible in spite of the fact that MacArthur knew Japanes landings could be expected at any time and had formed a pretty accurate idea of where the blow was most likely to fall. There was no mobile reserve, no early warning system, little artillery and what was left of the air force had been frittered away in opposing assaults recognised as subsidiary. The heaviest American bombers were no longer in the archipelago.

Yet as early as 18th December USAFFE Intelligence received reports of a large hostile convoy sailing southwards towards the Philippines. Early on the morning of the 20th the Navy reported that a large convoy had been seen about forty miles north of Lingayen Gulf. On the night of 20th/21st December units stationed in the area were given their first warning of the approaching enemy force.

Then on the morning of 21st December a party of Filipino soldiers near Bauang had watched amazed as a Japanese trawler cruised into Lingayen Gulf and, unhurriedly, took soundings before turning to travel north.

The force actually defending the long coastal front of the gulf consisted of two reserve divisions of the Philippine Army: the 11th and 21st – only one of which had artillery – plus some Philippine Scouts. The only coastal artillery was four 105mm guns of the 86th Field Artillery Battalion, Philippine Scouts, on the southern edge of the gulf. The eastern shore was held by the 11th Division, attached to which was the 71st Infantry, 71st Division, with only ten weeks training. Behind this direct path of the Japanese advance, was the 26th Cavalry, Philippine Scouts.

Only at Bauang, where the trawler had been spotted, were Filipino troops actually manning the beach defences. Armed with machine-guns they opened fire on the Kamajima Detachment as it came ashore. Despite heavy casualties the Japanese pressed on and the Filipinos were quickly forced to withdraw.

This was the entire land-based resistance to the landings, except for artillery fire from the guns of the Philippine Scouts. When units were sent to the scene they arrived too late to take effective action.

From the sea, the defence was equally ineffective if more determined. Hart's submarines which had been reserved for this very purpose were unable to get to close quarters with the transports in the shallows. One submarine which risked grounding itself to attack the convoys sank one of the *Maru* transports and then had to escape. All that the submarine defence proved was the impracticability of such a method as a means of stopping a seaborne force.

The most effective opposition came once more from the air. Planes which took off after the first reports of the landing had been received were augmented by the B-17s which, quite by coincidence, had been sent that day from Australia to attack targets in Davao. They flew north and, braving the strong fighter escort, strafed the landing transports and went on to hit the naval cover force. During the attack a battleship, first thought to be *Haruna*, flagship of Admiral Kondo's 2nd Fleet, but more probably Takahashi's flagship *Ashigara*, was hit and reported sunk. It was later discovered the report was untrue, though the Japanese, intercepting a radio message ordering a second attack, decided to take advantage of the low visibility to make an early escape, leaving the transports unprotected.

By this time, however, the leading waves were ashore. The 71st Infantry with a battery of 75mm guns attached was ordered during the day to move to engage the Tanaka Detachment to prevent the planned meeting with newly landed forces advancing towards it. The 71st Infantry was to achieve this by a frontal attack backed by a simultaneous attack on the left flank. But the Filipinos were unable to carry out the quick movement necessary, and were beaten back by the Kamajima Detachment, leaving the Japanese with a solid front.

As the day wore on the Japanese began to close in on their objectives and so far had encountered no major opposition. Units sent to oppose them were either too late, badly trained or lacking the spirit for the job, and were easily swept aside.

All this, however, was unknown to Homma who was aware only that his small force had much difficult terrain to cover and could be destroyed as soon as it emerged on to the Central Plain if the Americans and Filipinos were able to mount a concerted counterattack in their vastly superior numbers.

What was more, the greater part of his force was still aboard the transports with little likelihood of calmer seas in which the landing of the heavy artillery and other equipment could proceed.

He now had to decide, therefore, whether to order those ashore to consolidate where they were or to advance as originally planned. After a discussion among his staff, in which the more conservative minded were for consolidation, Homma decided to continue the advance and gave orders accordingly. But because of the weather late in the afternoon of 22nd December he instructed the convoy to move southwards to restart landing operations next morning.

Given this respite, Wainwright sought to muster his forces, bringing the 26th Cavalry, Philippine Scouts, and a small tank force from Weaver's Provisional Tank Group to stem the landings at Damortis by holding the coast road leading south. Only five of the tanks could be fuelled and sent forward in time and all these were hit by anti-tank fire. By evening the Japanese had taken Damortis.

With landing proceeding at the new point, resistance now focussed on the road junction at Rosario on which the Japs were advancing from two directions: inland and along the coast road, with the Cavalry fighting a delaying action until relieved by the 71st Division, Philippine Army, when they were sent to Binalonan to rest. It was a rest which was to prove very short lived.

Two battalions of the Homma's 47th Infantry moving south from Rosario struck the 71st Division's line near Sison. Reinforcements which USAFFE were sending up failed to arrive because a bridge they had to cross had been destroyed, forcing upon them a lengthy detour. During the delay this caused the Filipino line broke. They fled to the rear, leaving the guns exposed. With Japanese tanks and other units in full cry behind them they were swept back as far as Binalonan. Here on 24th Dec-

Above: Japanese tanks rumble forward past captured Filipinos. *Left:* US aircraft attack the enemy

ember the 27th Cavalry again engaged the Japs, and, though without anti-tank weapons, succeeded in stopping the attack and forcing the tanks to bypass the American position. By 0700 the 26th Cavalry had routed the infantry assault that followed and inflicted heavy casualties. The Scouts then counterattacked and the Japanese had to call for more tanks, but even with these were not able to make any progress. Then the 2nd Formosa were brought in to reinforce. With their arrival the 26th Cavalry were heavily outnumbered and, too deeply engaged to break off the action, were forced to fight on. By that afternoon the 26th Cavalry, its strength reduced from the 842 with which they had gone into battle to 450, was still fighting a delaying action while supply trains and their wounded were taken out of the town. At 1530 they began with-drawing and by dusk the 2nd Formosa began entering the town.

But that Christmas Day brought a fresh blow. Coincidentally with the departure of the Lingayen Gulf Task Force a second one commanded by Lieutenant-General Susumu Morioka,

commander of the 16th Division, had sailed from the Ryukyus. It was mak-ing the six-day voyage to Lamon Bay, south of Manila.

The force consisted of some 7,000 men of the 16th Division, with atta-ched service and other elements, including light armoured cars and field artillery.

For its landing, a most difficult site on the east side of Luzon had been chosen. Lamon Bay was subject to high winds in winter and the route of the advance to the west was blocked by the Tayabas Mountains. It had been picked in preference to the better landing sites on the west side of the islands, in Batangas Bay, only because the number of aircraft as-signed to the Philippine operation had been reduced by Southern Army and Lamon Bay gave the transports a shorter journey.

Morioka hoped to take the defenders by surprise, but was prepared to make an assault landing if necessary. His main aim, however, was to clear the beaches so as to avoid congestion and to advance across the mountains and concentrate for a possible counter-attack as rapidly as possible.

As in the Lingayen Gulf operation the landings were to be made at three points. Those here chosen were: Mauban, Atimonan and Siain, with the southernmost force taking Siain as soon as it could to cover the main advance.

In fact by choosing this less promis-ing landing site the Japanese had gained for themselves an advantage of which they were at the time unaware. General Parker's South Luzon Force, which was responsible for the defence of the area, had guarding the bay two batteries of six 155mm guns and a battalion of sixteen self-pro-pelled 75s. Parker had asked for ad-ditional artillery, but USAFFE, afraid of weakening the cover on the more obvious west coast, had refused the request. Thus, the place the Japanese had chosen to land was weaker in artillery cover than the one

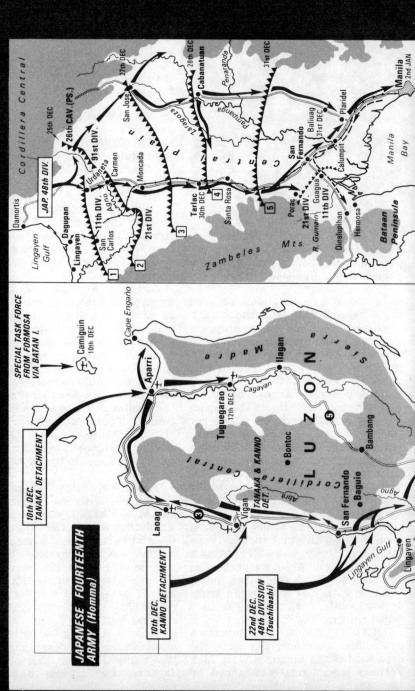

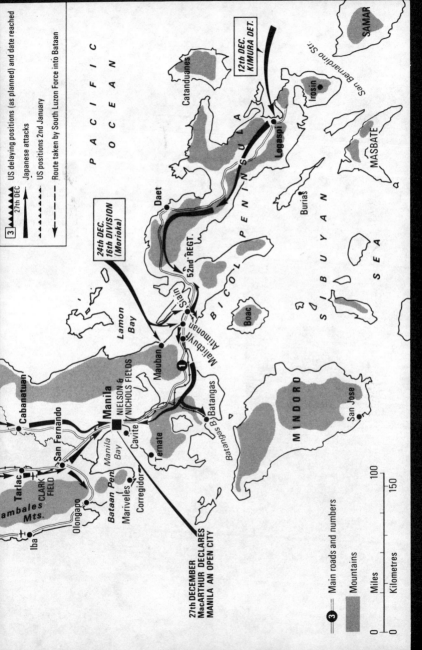

Japanese advances through Luzon

Japanese war-correspondant talks with successful tank commander

they had wanted to use.

On the night of 23rd/24th December, as the twenty-four transports carrying the invaders were moving into position ready for the onslaught, the defenders were in the process of moving several units from one place to another.

The only unit position was one drawn from the 1st Battalion, 1st Infantry Regiment – a unit of Philippine regulars – at Mauban, and at 2200 on the night of 23rd December they reported transports off Atimonan. At 0200 on the 24th troops were reported to be debarking at Siain. Then, two hours later, there were again reports of Japanese troops landing.

These reports, as had been the case at all previous Japanese landings, grossly exaggerated the size of the forces. As the Japanese troops began coming ashore, planes from the seaplane-carrier *Mizuho* started to attack, but the troops ran into heavy fire from the 2nd Battalion, 1st Infantry, which was dug in along the beach. American planes which strafed the landing craft also caused heavy casualties.

After fierce fighting the Philippine Army regulars were pushed back through Mauban village to a point five miles to the west, where they took up defensive positions and held the Japanese off.

In the meantime, the Siain force, landing without difficulty, had divided into two forces, one advancing along the Manila rail line, while the other moved southwards to try to join Colonel Kimura's forces from the earlier Legaspi landings, thus repeating what had been done at Lingayen and forming a solid line to protect the rear of the advance towards Manila. This group, however, encountered fierce opposition from General Jones' troops in the Bicol Peninsula and it was to be three days before they reached Kimura's force.

Morioka's men, too, caught by Jones' men, were held on the beaches so that as it came ashore, the second wave had to move round to the side to avoid action. It then struck off into the mountains, bypassing Atimonan which was taken at 1100 hours despite stubborn opposition from the Filipinos. Men of the 16th Reconnaissance Regiment in Morioka's landing force, with light bombers of the 8th Air Regiment attacking likely targets, then pushed up Route 1 and took the town of Malacbuy. The defenders, weakened by air attacks, had been forced back.

After the Japanese troops at Atimonan had finished mopping up they joined the main body at Malacbuy and together struck the defenders who were forced to withdraw under cover of darkness.

In this sector, at least, the Americans and Filipinos resisted with all the means and energy at their disposal. All the same, by dusk on Chrismas Eve the Japanese had completed the last difficult part of their landing operations at a cost of 84 dead and 184 wounded. They now had an unshakeable grip on North Luzon and were moving towards Manila. MacArthur's Philippine Army had failed to offer any consistently determined resistance.

General Homma had reason to be pleased with what his troops had achieved, not least the 16th Division whose prowess had surprised him. Its reputation had been a poor one and after a spell of fighting in China it had been brought back to Japan where, for some time, it had been in barracks in Osaka.

From north and south the Japanese troops were moving towards Manila, 100 miles away – the place where Homma expected the final battle to be fought. With the tactical advantage and the supremacy on sea and in the air he now possessed he was convinced the battle could only go one way. It was a smiling General Homma, therefore, who came ashore that evening on Philippine territory to set up headquarters for his Fourteenth Army at Bauang.

The Emerging Patterns

Now that the Japanese assault forces at Lamon Bay were in position, the pattern of their attacks, starting with the air-raids of the first day, was becoming clear to USAFFE. The lines of the pattern had been filled in with such ease that Homma must have regretted the dissipation of his already inadequate forces in the preliminary landings at Aparri, Vigan and Legaspi. He had paid his enemies the compliment of overestimating their powers of resistance.

His main ground forces were now advancing to catch MacArthur's troops in the pincer movement which

was to close upon Manila. It looked as if the defenders would be compelled to fight on the open territory of the Central Plain with the Japanese on either side. This, indeed, was the basis of the campaign plan, under which Homma had to achieve a decisive victory in the Philippines within fifty days, to allow his Fourteenth Army to be employed elsewhere in the continuing advance through southern Asia.

The trap, now ready to be sprung, was just what MacArthur had feared. As early as 12th December – the day of the Legaspi landings – MacArthur had mentioned to Quezon that if the Japanese landed in overwhelming strength it would be better to have the defending forces concentrated in Bataan rather than spread through the archipelago where the enemy could mop them up piecemeal. If the move to Bataan were made, the government, the office of the American High Commissioner, Francis Sayre, and the headquarters of USAFFE would be set up on Corregidor. This was the famous island-

Japanese bicycle troops take the road to Manila

Japanese bicycle troops advance during one of the lulls in fighting for the posession of Manila

fortress in Manila Bay, which the troops, convinced of its impregnability, called 'The Rock', mindful of that other bastion, the Rock of Gibraltar.

President Quezon was told that if such a move became necessary it might have to be made at as little as four hours notice and that, coincident with it, Manila would be declared an open city and abandoned to the Japanese.

The Philippine president, a man of small, typically Filipino build, plump, with quick, intelligent eyes, listened horrified to this news. His trepidation persisted, despite MacArthur's assurances that he was only preparing for the worst. Quezon's doubts are perhaps understandable. For over forty years he had been the voice of his people's freedom. Now sick with the tuberculosis which in a year or two

more was to kill him and living, like Roosevelt, in a wheelchair, it seemed to him that the dearly-won liberty of the Filipinos was to be meekly surrendered to the first challenger.

Perhaps the aversion the idea had aroused in Quezon prevented MacArthur from taking any active steps towards the move to Bataan. For even after the main Japanese invasion of 22nd December, the orders were still unchanged and Manila remained the centre of government and administration as well as USAFFE headquarters. In his despatches to Marshall in Washington, however, MacArthur indicated the move might be necessary. The strength of the Japanese landings was, in these reports, massively enlarged. Seventy to eighty transports were said to be involved and some 80,000-100,000 men supposed to have come ashore. At the same time MacArthur underestimated his own strength, claiming he had only about 40,000 men on Luzon. In fact the total number of troops there at that time

could not have been fewer than 75,000
80,000, while the total strength deployed against them was not more than 43,000 men.

He had reason to make his case good. He was proposing to return to War Plan Orange III, the very plan that he himself had quashed and which in any case, was intended to provide for a situation in which far weaker forces were in the Philippines. MacArthur had forces larger than any of his predecessors had dreamt of possessing, yet he was reverting to this defence plan.

MacArthur told Marshall he proposed to defend Bataan and 'hold' Corregidor. The Chief of Staff approved this plan and promised to do his utmost to send aid. In saying this, Marshall obviously intended primarily to give encouragement to MacArthur: the Japanese possessed mastery of sea and air and it was unlikely the navy would give its support to such a hazardous adventure taking them so far from their home bases. Marshall had, however, put in hand measures for a supply line to be opened to the Philippines via Australia and Java and ordered that 'no expense be spared' in the effort. Indeed, at that precise moment American officers in Australia were negotiating for ships for the run. It was, nonetheless, recognised that such a line could only provide a trickle and certainly not the massive influx of supplies and trained troops MacArthur seemed to have in mind. When no aid was forthcoming he was quick to criticise the navy for its lack of courage.

On 24rd December the Japanese had reached Rosario and MacArthur, somewhat belatedly, decided that the scheme for moving to Bataan should be put into effect. So far, perhaps to avoid demoralising the Filipinos further by letting them see preparations for a massive retreat, not the slightest preparation had been made. The only supplies so far in the peninsula had been put there under the exigencies of 'WPO-III' and were intended for the small force at that time planned. They include ammunition, 300,000 gallons of petrol, lubricating oil and greases as well as canned meat and fish. Apart from this MacArthur had had a general hospital built at Limay on the east coast, and plans had been made for a second.

On 24rd December Wainwright asked to withdraw south of the Agno River. This request seemed finally to galvanise MacArthur. That day all American commanders were notified, briefly, that 'WPO-III' was in effect. Next morning at a USAFFE staff conference Sutherland announced that the headquarters was to move to Corregidor. Because of the lateness with which action had been taken each man would be allowed to take only his field equipment and one suitcase or bedroll. The same afternoon Quezon, with High Commissioner Sayre, sailed to Corregidor in one of the island ferries.

At Naval headquarters Hart ordered

the only two destroyers left in Manila Bay to Java, where Rear-Admiral William A Glassford in *Marblehead* was trying to rally the Asiatic Fleet. Hart himself left for Java two days later in the submarine *Shark*, leaving only the tender *Canopus* and a handful of minesweepers, gunboats and motor torpedo boats, under Admiral Rockwell, in Manila Bay. They were to be used to cover the army's defence of Bataan.

Meanwhile, a depressing air of impending disaster was settling over Manila. In view of the speed with which evacuation had now to be carried out every available ship and barge was requisitioned and in brilliant moonlight they crossed to and from Bataan and Corregidor.

The mood of demoralisation in the city was heightened by demolition squads which were busy destroying anything which could be of use to the Japanese. An inverted cone of smoke rose from a fuel dump fire and spread in a pall over Manila as millions of gallons of fuel were destroyed.

The following morning, as the city went about its mournful Christmas Day, the Japanese flew over, dropping leaflets and strafing a passenger train, causing several casualties.

The tailing off in military activity in the capital was counterbalanced by increasing activity in Bataan. Troops and civilian workers were organising depots in the forests for a protracted defence, while docks were being established at Limay, Limao and Cabcaben and efforts were being made to improve the road network.

Engineers were erecting makeshift mills to grind the newly harvested rice into flour, abattoirs for the slaughter of animals were established wherever there was a running stream, beds were laid out for making salt from sea water, and fisheries organised.

All the time supplies were coming in so that by the end of Christmas Day it was reckoned that, thanks to the energetic efforts of the past forty-

eight hours, Bataan was, in the main essentials at least, supplied for a six month siege, though many things were not available or available only in limited quantities.

Troops, too, were beginning to arrive. On the 24th only the Philippine Division and a provisional air corps regiment were in the peninsula. Now, as others began to arrive they set about marking out new defence lines and digging themselves in. Under a regrouping of forces Wainwright, when he reached the peninsula, would be in command of the western sector of what hitherto had been the Bataan Defence Force, and now to become the I Philippine Corps. The eastern sector, to be called the II Philippine Corps, would be commanded by General Parker.

All these preparations, however, meant little unless all the American and Filipino troops at present scattered over the islands could be gathered in Bataan before the Japanese pincers closed. Crucial to this was the keeping open of Route 7, which turned north-westward from Route 3 out of Manila at Calumpit Bridge (in fact a pair of bridges) crossing the Pampang River south of San Fernando. It was along this route that the South Luzon Force would have to be withdrawn. This withdrawal would be slowed down as the force crossed the bridge. It would then have go northward a further ten miles before turning westward along Route 7 to enter Bataan. This meant that, at all costs, the North Luzon Force would all have to hold the Japanese back from San Fernando and Calumpit Bridge until the South Luzon Force was safely in the peninsula. If it failed MacArthur would lose half the men he was depending upon for the defence.

To cover their route of withdrawal would be the task of Wainwright's North Luzon Force, who were to fight a delaying action until their comrades from the south were estimated to be safe. Wainwright was to hold the Japanese along five defence lines across the Central Plain. These lines

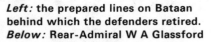

Left: the prepared lines on Bataan behind which the defenders retired.
Below: Rear-Admiral W A Glassford

Top left: USS Shark, which removed Admiral Hart from the Philippines. *Bottom left:* PT 32 was active in the Philippines. *Above:* damage to SS Marblehead. *Below:* USS Canopus remained behind in Manila Bay

Cautious Japanese tanks,
supported by infantry,
advance into unoccupied
Manila

had been drawn up before the war and were intended to make full use of natural defensive features. Each line was separated from the next by a distance estimated as a night's march. They terminated at each end on high ground and they covered Route 3 and Route 5, the two main approaches to Manila. To help hold the line MacArthur made available most of Weaver's Provisional Tank Group.

As the troops moved backwards, engineers, whose task had been to see that the roads and bridges were kept open, would seek to destroy them or make them impassable to the enemy.

The whole action was a complicated one, calling for exact timing and sacrificial courage on the part of those involved, but if it failed the whole plan for the defence of Bataan would founder.

One other major problem now remained: how to move the forces in the south into Bataan in the time available? This had been resolved by one of MacArthur's predecessors. Anticipating the logistic problems which might be encountered if a large force had to be moved quickly from one part of the island to another, and short of army transport, he had organised the commercial bus companies which operated the routes in Luzon into provisional motor transport battalions with company personnel as officers and men. Thus, while civilian travellers found themselves bereft of transport, the buses, decorated with the gaudy brilliance of which Orientals alone are capable, joined incongruously with the army trucks and every other vehicle in a day and night shuttle ser-

It was on the day that Manila became an open city that Homma's Intelligence chief, Lieutenant-Colonel Yoshio Nakajima, reported the first evidence of the removal of MacArthur's headquarters to Corregidor and the transfer of some army units to Bataan. Homma decided, rightly, that MacArthur planned to fight a delaying action through Bataan and Corregidor. Since, however, his own mission was to take Manila, the general opinion among Fourteenth Army Headquarters' Staff was that they should pursue this task with their main forces and not allow themselves to be sidetracked. Indeed, some staff officers present felt that MacArthur's 'sideslip' was assisting them towards completion of their task. MacArthur's army was, in one Japanese officer's phrase, 'a cat entering a sack'.

All the same, for the Japanese to reach their objective – Manila – they would have to fight their way past Wainwright's North Luzon Force, which was determined on a tenacious holding action. The strong resistance put up by the 26th Cavalry had so far stopped the Japanese from crossing the Agno River, but by noon on Christmas Day, in a massed attack, they defeated the Philippine Army units defending the right of the line and occupied the town of Urdaneta. The Americans were then forced back on the second of their five lines of retreat, that on the far bank of the river. The pressure continued and by the 26th the Japanese crossed the river at two points, at one almost cutting off part of the 11th Division being evacuated from Carmen by rail. Only a hastily improvised road-block, composed of a 75mm half-track and three tanks, held the Japanese infantry hurrying down Route 3 to cut off the Filipinos at Moncada and saved the situation. By the night of the 27th Wainwright pulled back to his fourth defence line, stretching across the plain from Tarlac in the west to Cabanatuan in the east, and about sixty miles from Manila.

vice carrying goods, equipment, ammunition, medical supplies and men to Bataan.

On 27th December, while this movement was taking place, MacArthur took the next step: that of officially declaring Manila an open city. The proclamation, drawn up in consultation with Washington, was published in the papers and broadcast on Manila radio. From that day the black-out of the city ceased. But the declaration failed to bring the hoped-for relief from Japanese bombing and now, without even the out-of-date anti-aircraft guns to keep them at high altitude, they struck where they chose. The Intendencia Buildings, the College of San Juan de Latran, the Church of Santo Domingo, Santa Rosa College, Santa Catalina College, some of the oldest colonial buildings in Asia, were destroyed and hundreds of civilians killed.

The Japanese watch the South Luzon Force retire into Bataan

Under the agreed plan of the withdrawal Wainwright was to hold each line just long enough to force the enemy to prepare for a major attack, then step back. The aim was to delay, not to defeat the Japanese. All the same Wainwright decided to fight it out on the Tarlac-Cabanatuan line as this would give the South Luzon Force more time and a wider clearance for their movements. On 28th December, however, the Japanese started a determined advance from the Agno River, with tanks of the 4th and 7th Regiments forming the spearhead. As the tanks approached Cabanatuan men of the 47th Infantry began crossing the river under an artillery barrage. The defenders found themselves outflanked and on the night of 29th December, with tanks leading, the Japs entered Cabanatuan.

On the 30th they continued the pressure with their 48th Division, supported by mountain and heavy field artillery, pursuing the withdrawing Philippine 91st Division. The defenders crossed the Penaranda River, destroyed the steel bridge and then tried to form a hasty rearguard made up of some sixty-five Filipino soldiers of the 92nd Infantry Regiment, supported by 300 boys from cadet forces of Manila schools, who had just reached the line. The Japanese broke through without difficulty.

Now forced back on a shortened fifth and final line, the defenders awaited the next attack which came as elements of the Kanno Detachment, on cycles, approached the American lines quite openly. They were spotted by American tanks and forced back with a loss of eighty-two men.

Forced to withdraw once more as the pressure increased, the Americans now crossed the Zaragoza River, another of the streams criss-crossing the plain, and lost some of their precious tanks as well as part of 11th Division when nervous engineers blew the bridge over the river too soon.

At the western end of the same line, too, the Japanese were making progress. South of Tarlac the Philippine 21st Division, untried in battle, was attacked by the Kamajima Detachment and by the 30th Tarlac was lost. In a second attack, however, the Philippine defenders held their ground and inflicted heavy losses which included the killing of Colonel Kamajima himself.

A fierce and determined action by the artillery of the 21st Division, under its American instructor, First Lieutenant Carl J Savoie, slowed down the pursuit and successfully covered the withdrawal of the 21st Division, but by the 31st the Japanese were within thirty miles of Manila.

This advance exposed the right flank of the forces pulling out of South Luzon and MacArthur saw that he must at all costs cover them at the point at which they wheeled to enter Bataan – when they would be at their most vulnerable. To do this it was crucial to hold the area round the Calumpit Bridge. MacArthur placed every unit that could be spared along a line about five miles south of Pampanga in the Baliuag-Plaridel area. On the 30th the Japanese were reported marching towards Plaridel and by the 31st had reached the outskirts of Baliuag. Here they encountered unexpected resistance and withdrew. By mid-afternoon, however, the Japanese had massed an overwhelming force in front of the town. To hold them, all available tanks in Weaver's Provisional Tank Group were sent to attack and fought a pitched battle in which eight Japanese tanks were destroyed.

The line held just long enough. By 0500 on 1st January the last units crossed the Calumpit Bridge and were safely on their way to Bataan. Almost unbelievably, particularly in view of their now unchallenged air superiority, the Japanese made no attempt to destroy the vital bridge at Calumpit. At 0615 that morning it was blown by Wainwright's engineers.

The Capital Occupied

It was not the first time in their long history that the Philippines had known the menaces of Japan. In the 16th Century, under the leadership of the expansionist Shogun, Toyotomi Hideyoshi, an attempt had been made to take the islands. Spanish diplomacy – and blood money – had forestalled it, but tension again reached breaking point some years later and the islands were only saved from attack by Hideyoshi's death in 1598.

Masaharu Homma, like his overlord Tojo and his fellow-militarists in Tokyo, saw himself as the successor to the legendary *samurai* Hideyoshi, and his bid to bring the Philippines under Imperial domination was not to be bought off with a few thousand Spanish doubloons.

All the same, when it came to the actual occupation of the capital city Homma seemed to be in no hurry. The Japanese had acknowledged the open city declaration as early as 26th December in a broadcast on Radio Tokyo and by 31st December details of the declaration were in the possession of Fourteenth Army Headquarters which Homma had now established at Cabanatuan. Still no move was made.

The city had prepared itself for the Japanese entry. Mayor Jorge Vargas had taken all possible steps to see that the coming of the occupiers was peaceful and that there should be no grounds for retaliatory measures. Round the outskirts, at strategic points, notices had been placed reading, 'OPEN CITY! NO SHOOTING!'

The last of USAFFE headquarters staff had gone. The fuel dump fires, now smouldering out, had left dark clouds in the sky and a fine patina of ash, like dry snow, which settled on everything. To add to this there was the smell of rotting garbage in the streets, for despite the injunction to everyone involved in local administration to stay at their posts, there had been no collection for days past and many local officials had packed their bags and gone to Bataan or Corregidor.

Yet that day a strange and heady atmosphere came upon the city as the guns fell silent. It was as though it had suddenly become an enclave out of time and the events of war. Hotels, restaurants and night clubs opened for New Year's Eve celebrations. There were dances and balls and women put on their evening dresses.

As the bells pealed and the crackers burst at midnight there was another sound: the smashing of glass as bartenders broke bottles of whisky to prevent them falling into Japanese hands.

The next morning the American quartermaster's stores were thrown open and looting Filipinos had a field day helping themselves to everything inside, especially the large stocks of frozen foods.

Still there was no sign of the Japanese, though Lieutenant-General

Despite being declared an open city, the Japanese still bombed Manila

Tsuchibashi, commander of the 48th Division, had in fact asked Homma's permission that day to enter the city with a force of 2,000 men and extra editions of the newspapers announced that Japanese occupation was imminent.

On 2nd January looting continued, but by late afternoon permission to occupy was given and Major-General Koichi Abe, commander of the 48th Division's infantry group, led one battalion of the 1st Formosa Regiment and two of the 47th Infantry into the city.

The triumphal cavalcade was watched only by a curious few. All were silent. As the procession passed Japanese soldiers moved among the few bystanders handing out propaganda leaflets seeking the cooperation of the Manilans in 'crushing Anglo-American Imperialism'.

For the arriving emissaries of His Imperial Majesty the Mikado the reception was a disappointment. They had expected to be welcomed as liber-

Above: General Homma and Mayor Vargas meet in the capital for the first time. *Right:* the first Japanese troops finally march into the Philippines' capital city

ators from the American yoke, but few people even bothered to look at the leaflets and those who did saw them only as souvenirs of occupation to be brought out and shown in years to come to inquisitive offspring.

The small occupying force immediately placed guards on all strategic points, while Japanese civilians, just released from the internment camps round the city, acted as interpreters.

Within a few hours American and British civilians in Manila were being rounded up and those who, two days earlier, had been among the gay and colourful revellers at the New Year's Eve balls, were now led to a camp hastily improvised in the field at Santo Tomas University. By that night the only Europeans still free were Germans, Italians and Spaniards.

The next day restaurants and bars were closed and the few stores open found themselves doing flourishing business with Japanese officers buying all they could pay for with the occupation scrip.

Two days later Homma proclaimed the establishment of a Japanese Military Administration which would supervise the economic and cultural affairs of the city. Its director-general was named as Major-General Yoshide Hayashi. At the same time a series of stringent orders was issued: there was to be a curfew and a blackout; martial law was proclaimed; all firearms, munitions and war materials were to be handed in; any hostile act against the Japanese Military Administration or its personnel would be punished by death; for every Japanese killed ten Filipinos would be executed; use of radio transmitters was forbidden and all radio sets were 'reconditioned' to receive only Japanese or Jap-sponsored stations.

All industries, factories, banks, schools, churches and printing presses were brought under Japanese control and the flying of the Filipino flag or the singing of the National Anthem forbidden.

Shortly after his arrival in the city, Homma summoned Vargas to him and explained that he himself, his Emperor and his compatriots had watched with the greatest sympathy and admiration the struggles of their brother-Asiatics to free themselves from American dominance. Now had come the time to co-operate with Japan in building an Asia for Asiatics. He ended by ordering Vargas to form a government to replace the 'American puppet' Quezon-Osmeña Government which had abdicated its responsibilities.

On 23rd January Vargas named, in what was later to be called 'The Charter of Treason', his new government. It contained many prominent Filipinos. Among them were edu-

Left: Japanese troops watch burning Manila from the bay. *Above:* alert Japanese forces await resistance

cationalist, writer and lawyer, José Laurel; the satirist and politician Clara Recto; and the landowner economist José Yulo, a former Chief Justice of the Philippine Supreme Court. That same day the Philippine Executive Commission was formed with Vargas as chairman. Each of its departments was given Japanese 'advisers'.

Five days earlier Manuel Quezon, whose Nacionalista Party had been returned with an overwhelming majority in the elections, had, with his Vice-President, Osmeña, been given the oath of office for a further four year period. The ceremony took place in Malinta Tunnel, that complex of catacombs under Corregidor island in which both MacArthur's headquarters and the government-in-exile were housed.

Simultaneously, fifteen miles from the entrance to Bataan, the North Luzon Force was fighting the last of its delaying actions, endeavouring to give the troops now regrouping time to establish a line.

Along a ten mile front between Guagua and Porac Wainwright had mustered the 11th and 21st Divisions as well as some armour and cavalry. The 26th Cavalry which had distinguished itself earlier was just to the rear as a reserve. The troops were convinced they were about to face the entire Japanese force in the island, estimated at more than 120,000 men. In fact, only two reinforced regiments with tanks and artillery confronted them.

Homma, however, had now issued orders for the taking of the Guagua-Porac line. A detachment called the Takahashi Detachment, after its commander, Lieutenant-Colonel Katsumi Takahashi, was to cut through at Porac and advance to Dinalupihan, the road junction just south of the border between Pampanga and Bataan

Left: handouts from the occupiers.
Above: Japanese Propaganda Section

provinces. A second force, mainly
derived from the 48th Division, and
led by Colonel Tanaka was to drive
through Guagua to Hermosa which
also stood on the roads leading into
Bataan. The attack was scheduled for
0200 on 2nd January.

Homma expected a quick and easy
victory which would bring his campaign to an end well within the fifty
days apportioned to it.

When the attackers struck the
21st Infantry, however, they were
held without difficulty and plans were
even made by 21st Infantry divisional
headquarters for a counterattack,
but this was stopped by darkness.
Through the night the Filipino artillery men kept up unremitting inter-
dictory fire and it was found, before
the delayed counterattack began,
that the Japanese had already withdrawn.

They returned, this time supported

by heavy artillery and aircraft, and
under this the line broke and the
Japanese advance was carried so far
beyond its objectives that the 21st
Infantry was ordered 'hold the line or
die where you are'. The Filipino
commanders did their best, but they
had already been deprived of some of
their troops sent southward to Guagua
where a fight was in progress, and
when Takahashi launched an assault
against the 21st Infantry at noon it
cut through on the left. Takahashi
pushed forward immediately and advanced with such speed that at one
time the whole 21st Infantry staff was
nearly captured in its command post.
By night, however, the remorseless
fire of the defending artillery again
brought the advance to a halt. The
truth was that the artillery had so far
upset the Japanese plans that their
assaults were turned into cautious
probes as they themselves tried to
bring up their artillery. Their 105mm
guns, emplaced on high ground, did
fire upon the rear areas but because of

95

poor markmanship caused little damage.

Nor was this Homma's only concern. On 2nd January Imperial General Headquarters, Tokyo, told him the whole timetable for the invasion of Java had been advanced by a month. Because of this his 48th Division, which was not to have gone to Sixteenth Army until the end of the Philippine campaign, was wanted right away and with it the 5th Air Group. In its place he was to receive a brigade, the 65th, commanded by Lieutenant-General Akira Nara, with a strength of 6,500 men. Thus, at the time he was about to embark on a vital battle he found himself involved in a changeover of units and a reduction in the number of men available. Worse still, the 65th Brigade had been raised only a year before as a garrison unit, and was made up largely of enlisted men with only a month's training. Its three infantry regiments – the 122nd, 141st and 142nd – contained only two battalions each. There were few vehicles and no field artillery.

These troops arrived on 1st January and were moved at once to the Tarlac area, ready to be pushed into the battle.

They were not, however, needed. Because of the continuous pressure on the Guagua end of the line Wainwright ordered the 21st to pull back to the Gumain River, about eight miles south of Porac, to keep the line intact. During the night the withdrawal was carried out successfully, though amid some confusion. Strangely, as at Calumpit Bridge, the Japanese did not take advantage of the situation to strafe the defenders.

The withdrawal into Bataan was now complete and on that day, 2nd January, MacArthur announced this successful retreat. The rearguards of

the North Luzon Force had done their work and lines were being formed in the peninsula itself. In the evacuation not one major unit had been lost and only once, at Cabanatuan, had the defence line failed to hold for long enough to allow the planned withdrawal to take place.

This is not to say the movement had been executed without cost. Both sides had paid dearly. The Japanese losses were much higher than they had bargained for and certainly far more than Homma, with his limited forces, could afford. Their total casualties since the landings had been 2,000, including 627 killed, 1,282 wounded and seven missing.

Wainwright's force of 28,000 men had lost some 12,000. These losses were caused, in the main, less from combat casualties than from the desertion of Filipino soldiers.

The important thing, all the same,

US Marines on the move within the Bataan defence system

was that the South Luzon Force, under the command of General Jones since 24th December, when Parker had gone to Bataan, was now safe and available as a defensive unit. Only a thousand of its 15,000 men had been lost in the retreat. For the first time since the beginning of hostilities the Japanese had been out-manoeuvred. Though they might now occupy the 'free city' of Manila, the use of Manila Bay itself was denied them so long as the Americans held Bataan and Corregidor.

Then men reaching Bataan were tired and hungry and they knew they faced a gruelling and probably lengthy struggle. Despite all the efforts that had been made many items of equipment, some of them vital, were in short supply. For example, there were

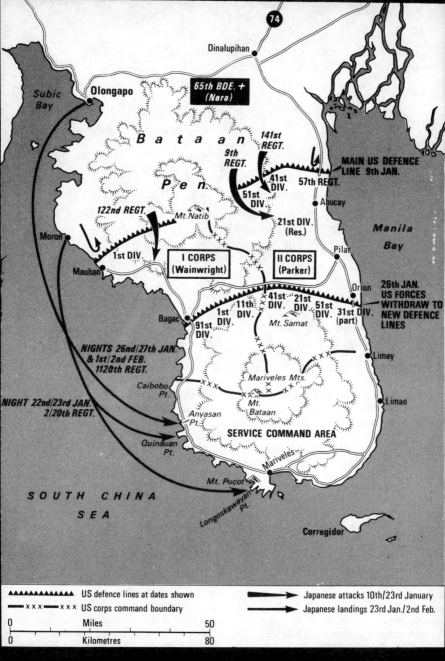

74

Dinalupihan

Subic Bay

Olongapo

65th BDE. +
(Nara)

B a t a a n

141st
REGT.

9th
REGT.

MAIN US DEFENCE
LINE 9th JAN.

P e n.

41st
DIV.

57th REGT.

51st
DIV.

122nd REGT.

Mt. Natib

Abucay

Manila
Bay

21st DIV.
(Res.)

Moron

1st DIV.

I CORPS
(Wainwright)

II CORPS
(Parker)

Pilar

Mauban

41st
DIV.

21st
DIV.

Orion

26th JAN.
US FORCES
WITHDRAW TO
NEW DEFENCE
LINES

Bagac

11th
DIV.

1st
DIV.

51st
DIV.

31st DIV.
(part)

91st
DIV.

Mt. Samat

NIGHTS 26th/27th JAN.
& 1st/2nd FEB.
1120th REGT.

Limay

Caibobo
Pt.

Mariveles Mts.

Limao

NIGHT 22nd/23rd JAN.
2/20th REGT.

Anyasan
Pt.

Mt.
Bataan

Quinauan
Pt.

SERVICE COMMAND AREA

Mariveles

S O U T H   C H I N A

Mt. Pucot

S E A

Longoskawayan
Pt.

Corregidor

▲▲▲▲▲▲▲▲▲ US defence lines at dates shown	➤ Japanese attacks 10th/23rd January
━xxx━ ━xxx━ US corps command boundary	➤ Japanese landings 23rd Jan./2nd Feb.

0   Miles   50

0   Kilometres   80

The defence of Bataan Peninsula begins

no mosquito nets and very little quinine. Malaria was already becoming a problem and would grow steadily worse as other shortages took their toll of men's physical resistance. These deficiencies were the result of the hurried and belated way in which the defence of the peninsula had been organised.

There were now some 80,000 troops in Bataan, as well as some 26,000 civilians who had fled there. (Shrewdly, Homma had seen the advantages of increasing the population of the peninsula and ordered his officers to put no impediment in the way of refugees making their way there.) With a population this size the food and other resources originally estimated as sufficient for a six month siege could only last a much shorter time.

It was now calculated that food stocks on Bataan were enough for 100,000 men for thirty days, and for this reason MacArthur had already ordered civilians to be placed on half rations, equivalent to 2,000 calories a day.

Among the defence forces were the motor torpedo boats and minesweepers left by the Asiatic Fleet – and now, together with the 4th Marines, placed under MacArthur's direct control, Weaver's tanks, and a few P-40s. In addition, engineers were working round the clock with civilian aid trying to build two fields from which the aircraft could operate.

In terms of ground forces on Bataan, MacArthur had the Philippine Division, two regular Philippine Army Divisions and seven Philippine Army reserve divisions.

The area they would have to defend was a strip of land twenty-five miles long and twenty miles at its widest point. Down it, like a spine, ran two ranges of mountains covered in forest and jungle, the second of which had peaks rising to 4,700 feet. Between the two ranges was a narrow valley, crossed by streams and there were narrow coastal plains on either side of the mountains, down which the main highways ran.

MacArthur had placed his I Corps, which included one Philippine regular division, and two reserve divisions and other units on the left and the II Corps, with four Philippine army Divisions, and elements of the Philippine Division on the right. At the tip of the peninsula a Service Command Area had been designated. Here the 2nd Regular Division and the 71st Division, which had been badly depleted, were in readiness.

The first of the main lines of resistance ran from Mauban, on the South China Sea coast, to Abucay, on the shores of Manila Bay. Should it be necessary the defenders could drop back into a reserve line some six miles to the rear. A third projected line crossed the Mariveles Mountains, the highest part of the peninsula. And still further back was Corregidor, separated from Bataan by a two mile wide channel. This would serve as the supply base for the Bataan defence and would at the same time deny the Japanese the use of Manila harbour, even if they took the peninsula itself.

The morale of the men was high, probably higher than it had been since the beginning of the battle. Though they had so far been unsuccessful in their efforts to fend off the aggressor they believed that here at last they were in a place they could hold out and perhaps, in the end, strike back. Rumours of massive reinforcements from the US kept circulating among the men who became more and more convinced that success was only a matter of their hanging on for relief.

They knew, too, that the terrain of Bataan was well known to MacArthur, and that here he would be pitting his wits against the Japanese on more equal terms. Their superiority in air power, tanks and artillery would give them a somewhat less than overwhelming advantage.

Bataan: The First Round

Though he had encountered some setbacks, Homma still did not anticipate great difficulty in taking Bataan. This optimism was largely based on the estimates he was receiving from his own Intelligence group which put the number of men there at about 25,000 when actually there were about three times as many. He had also been led to believe that both the men's morale and their physical condition were poor and that large scale desertions were taking place. (There was, of course, some basis for this last

suggestion.) Basing his plans on these reports, Homma expected the ensuing battle to be one of pursuit rather than assault. The operation was to be a simple advance down the two highways on either side of the peninsula and much of the fighting would be done by Akira Nara's 65th Brigade, which was to replace the 48th Division.

To the 65th were attached field and mountain artillery, as well as the tanks of the 7th Tank Regiment. Giving air support was an army air unit under Colonel Komataro Hoshi consisting of eleven fighters, thirty-six light bombers and reconnaissance, artillery observation and liaison aircraft.

Nara's attack on the eastern side, against the II Corps, was to be made by the 141st Infantry Regiment, accompanied by mountain artillery, anti-tank guns and engineers, while against the I Corps, on the west, he sent a combat team built round the

Japanese armour advances against the defenders of Bataan

The Japanese Type 95 (1935) 'Kyo-Go' Light Tank saw service in the South East Asia and Pacific campaigns. Produced from 1935 to 1945, it was the last type of Japanese light tank to see active service. The fighting compartment was extremely cramped, the armour plate thin, but the Type 95 was well provisioned with vision slits and positions for light machine guns to provide all-round defence. It was no match for Allied anti-tank weapons or tanks. *Weight:* 8½ tons. *Crew:* three. *Armament:* one 37mm gun and two 7.7mm light machine guns. *Armour:* 6 to 12 mm. *Speed:* 28mph. *Engine:* 6-cylinder air-cooled diesel, 110hp

122nd Infantry Regiment. This second unit was to advance westward across the neck of the peninsula to Olongapo, turn southwards to Moron, then advance to Bagac which formed the western terminus of the only lateral road crossing Bataan. Nara did not expect resistance until he reached this point and was not even sure he would meet it here.

At noon of 4th January the 65th Brigade began moving down Route 74 to relieve the 48th Division and to start the attack on Bataan proper. At 1500 on 9th January, the Japanese began their assault with a heavy artillery barrage against II Corps defending the right. It was the first of

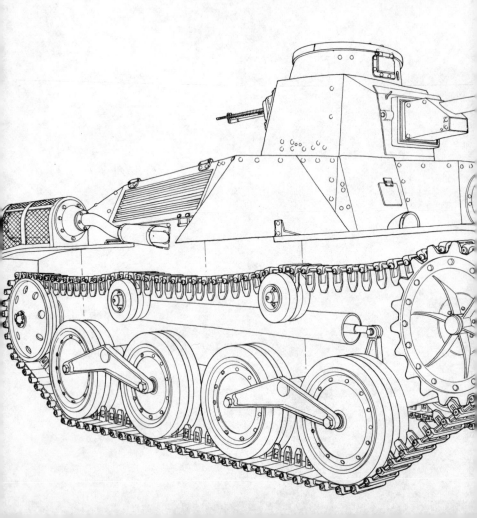

many such barrages the defenders were to experience and which the veterans were to compare with those in France in the First World War.

Homma's Intelligence, however, had erred not only in estimating the strength and morale of the enemy, but also in calculating the position of the main defence line. The Japanese advanced into thin air only to be brought up short as they, in turn, were subjected to a devastating bombardment.

On the western side, too, they found themselves advancing unopposed against a purely imaginary foe and were led to conclude that the Americans had withdrawn over a wide area.

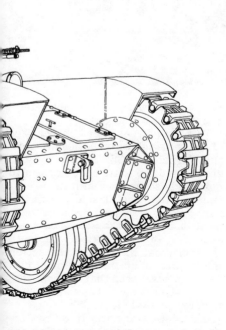

Actually the Japanese had simply not reached the main defence line.

On the morning of 10th January MacArthur and Sutherland crossed from Corregidor to see the position for themselves. This was to be the only visit MacArthur made to his troops during the whole campaign, a fact which later led to much libellous comment when these troops were fighting their last ditch stand, and felt themselves deserted by their commander. The suggestion of cowardice implicit in such criticisms was, of course, without foundation for, when Corregidor came under heavy Japanese air attack, MacArthur showed that he could behave with considerable coolness and courage. Nevertheless, his absence from Bataan left a deep bitterness among his men.

The day of his visit was the very one on which Homma had inadvertently chosen to address his first surrender demand. 'You are well aware you are doomed,' his note read. 'The end is near. The question is how long you will be able to resist?' It went on persuasively to praise the courage and fighting spirit of the troops, urging surrender to 'avoid needless bloodshed', while promising that the Japanese offensive would be continued 'with inexorable force which will bring you only disaster'.

Shortly afterwards, the Filipino troops, thought by the Japanese to be on the verge of collapse, were subjected to a separate appeal to surrender and build a 'new Philippines for and by Filipinos'.

The only response these missives called forth was an increase in artillery fire. What troubled the USAFFE commander and his Chief of Staff, when they returned to Corregidor, was not the surrender demands, but the discovery that the two corps commanders had left the inland flanks of their lines comparatively weak, in the belief that the enemy would be unable to strike through the dense mountains and jungle which covered the terrain of central Bataan.

The following day Parker and Wainwright were specifically ordered to extend their lines until they joined.

On the night of 10/11th January the Japanese made their first contact with the main resistance line and the 57th Infantry Regiment, Philippine Scouts in II Corps' sector came under heavy attack. The 2nd Battalion of Nara's 141st Infantry had reached a canefield which had been left standing about 1,500 yards in front of the line. At midnight the Japanese began a *banzai* attack with wave after wave coming at the defenders. Men of the leading waves threw themselves on the barbed wire in the face of point blank fire from 75mm guns, forming a bridge of corpses over which subsequent waves could pass.

This attack continued in the face of heavy slaughter on both sides until the defenders were forced to give ground and the units next to them to pull back so as to maintain a continuous line. The attack was finally halted when reserves were sent up to meet it. At dawn the Scouts counterattacked and penetrated almost to their original line. When the action was broken off on the morning of 12th January it was seen that the Japanese had lost between two and three hundred in dead alone.

Elsewhere along the line the Japanese had infiltrated, but during the morning these pockets were mopped up, though they caused some casualties among the Scouts. The net result of the attacks had been negligible advances and heavy losses for the Japanese.

In the west they had been even less successful. They were unable to make progress against the 31st Division in I Corps sector and began probing along the line hoping to find a soft spot. Other units moving through central Bataan were delayed by the thick jungle.

It was now obvious to the Japanese that the taking of the peninsula was not going to be the easy operation they had hoped for. They were suffering, too, particularly in this land of stream and jungle, from the fact that they had no large scale maps. Added to this was the extreme difficulty in

Left: **Japanese troops cutting their way through the wire defences.** *Below:* **a forward observation post**

maintaining communications. Signals detachments were inexperienced and often got lost in the jungle. Consequently a unit would often have no idea of the intentions or even the location of supporting units. In the end Nara was forced to change all his plans. He now committed a third regiment, the 9th Infantry, and issued a fresh set of battle instructions which would do precisely what Sutherland feared: strike at the inland flank of Parker's II Corps sector, then turn eastward to take the line from the rear.

In the next few days the Japanese made renewed preparations which included the bringing up of fresh artillery. The whole American line felt itself under pressure and early on 13th January, the day on which Nagra's offensive was to begin, elements of the 21st Division, Philippine Army, counterattacked to meet a developing threat to the eastern anchor of the line round Abucay. They

successfully pushed the Japanese
back and prevented the launching of
an offensive at this point.

Because of growing danger elsewhere, however, Parker was forced to
ask for reinforcements. The request
came as no surprise to USAFFE in
view of their criticisms of the state of
his inland flanks, and they at once
despatched one of the best units they
had, the Philippine Division, consisting of one American and one Philippine Scout regiment.

While these were on their way,
Parker proposed to use the 51st
Division to counterattack on the
morning of 16th January. The divisional commander at once protested that
a premature and unsupported counterattack was too risky. All the same,
the attack went ahead at dawn on the
16th, and at once ran into fierce resistance from the Japanese who had

**The attackers bring up more men to
test the defenders strength**

106

been expecting it. One unit, however, did manage to advance, but, in doing so, pushed so far ahead of those on either side that it created an opening which the Japanese were quick to exploit. Elements of the 141st Infantry were infiltrated into one corner of the gap while the 9th Infantry pressed in on the other corner. There was now the risk of a double envelopment. The entire line held by the 51st gave way under the pressure, the Filipinos flying rearwards in disorder. As the Japanese, after a brief respite, returned to the attack, the units on either side of the gap in the now torn defensive line, were forced to withdraw to protect their own flanks. The 43rd Infantry Regiment, Philippine Army, held against repeated attacks, but other elements of the Japanese 9th Infantry were making deep inroads in the mountains further west, threatening an envelopment of the

entire II Corps line.

On 22nd January Sutherland arrived in Bataan, on MacArthur's orders, to see the situation at first hand. His first stop was at General Parker's II Corps headquarters at Limay and though he went from there to Wainwright's headquarters he had in fact already made up his mind that the Abucay-Mauban battle line would have to be abandoned and the troops pulled back to new positions – which had already been prepared in case of further withdrawals – behind the Pilar-Bagac road.

This was the only possible decision since the disintegration of the 51st Division, coupled with the failure of the Philippines Division when it reached the battle zone, to restore the original line, had provided a broad breach through which the enemy was pouring, threatening both I and II Corps.

The position was made still more difficult by the fact that the Japanese penetrations in Wainwright's sector had enabled them to establish a roadblock along the West Road.

The withdrawal was accordingly approved by MacArthur, who reported on the situation in a pessimistic dispatch to Washington. His losses were high and represented about thirty-five per cent of his total force while some units had lost as much as sixty per cent. Along the new and shorter line, MacArthur said he planned to 'fight it out to complete destruction' and he nominated Sutherland as his successor if he should be killed.

Orders were given and the withdrawal began amid scenes of the greatest confusion as the troops streamed down every available road. There were no military police to control traffic and with every semblance of organisation breaking down the principal concern of commanders was that the Japanese might begin an artillery

MacArthur pays his only visit to Bataan Peninsula. His absence from the scene tended to alienate him from his troops

bombardment of the road junctions – which would certainly have turned the retreat into a rout. Fortunately, the Japanese once more failed to take advantage of an opportunity.

While the withdrawal was taking place the Japanese attacks on the Philippine Division continued and reached their climax on the night of 23/24th January as the men were moving eastward toward Abucay and the main road. The thin rearguard line held just long enough to permit the bulk of the troops to get out. Early on the morning of 25th the last Americans, under artillery and tank cover, staggered out of their positions. They looked in the words of one observer like 'walking dead men'.

The withdrawal continued all through the night of 24th January, with the Japanese in full pursuit. During the 25th the Japanese air force took over, bombing and strafing the troops and causing particularly devastating casualties among the untrained Filipino soldiers.

On the morning of 25th January the men of II Corps began to take their places in the new line under tank cover.

The withdrawal of I Corps was more orderly as moves towards it had been made earlier.

The Japs had forced the Americans off their first line of resistance, but only at high cost to themselves. The three infantry regiments of Nara's 65th Brigade which entered the battle on 9th January with a strength of 6,651 officers and men, had, by the 24th, suffered 1,472 combat casualties, while its attached units had probably lost men proportionately.

By the end of the struggle for the Abucay line Nara was writing that his brigade had reached the 'extreme stages of exhaustion.'

His efforts, however, had not been restricted to frontal attack. Just after the offensive against the Abucay-Maubar line began Homma expressed concern at the resistance and suggested that, to bring about a greater dispersion of American forces, landings might be attempted at various points along the western coast of Bataan. As Wainwright's resistance hardened, Major-General Naoki Kimura, whose 16th Division was engaged in the drive down the West Road, decided to attempt landings at three points, behind I Corps' front. Landing barges had already been brought from Lingayen to Olongapo for the purpose and he knew that the rugged coastline of Bataan was difficult to defend.

Furthermore, the American troops entrusted with the task were largely a scratch force. They included the 1st Regiment Philippine Constabulary and a 'Naval Battalion' under Francis J Bridget, a grounded Catalina pilot. His unit was made up of ground crews and fliers from the now defunct Patrol Wing 10, as well as

sailors from *Canopus* and the Mariveles Naval Base and some sixty Marines. Artillery included two 75mm guns, a battery of 3-inch guns, four 6-inch naval guns, only two of which were so far emplaced. Their small arms were made up of a variety of weapons, including some First World War machine-guns, and many of the troops of this assorted force had never even fired a rifle. A further bizarre touch was added by their uniforms, which were of a variegated mustard colour, the result of an unsuccessful attempt to dye their blue naval uniforms khaki. Together with the other defence forces they were under the command of Brigadier-General Clyde A Selleck.

For the landing Kimura chose the 2nd Battalion, 20th Infantry. On 22nd

January they embarked from Moron to land at Caibobo Point on the east coast. Once more the Japs felt the effect of their lack of maps. The only ones they possessed were so small in scale that it was impossible to pick out single points, particularly as in this region the coastline merges into the dark background of the mountains, making the identification of headlands difficult even in daylight for an experienced seaman using adequate charts. Shortly after setting out the invading force found the going hard. The sea was rough and the leading barges ran into an American torpedo boat which sank one of them. However, it was unaware there were others and went on its way.

Then, about half an hour later, it encountered another and damaged it irreparably. Before the barge sank a boarding party took several prisoners and captured a dispatch case of documents.

These untoward events meant that the invasion flotilla had now lost its bearings and was divided into two groups, so that no one reached the intended landing point. One group of about a third of the battalion landed at Longoskawayan Point, ten miles beyond the objective, and the other, made up of an assortment of troops and attached units, reached Quinauan Point. At both places they found themselves on undefended beaches.

The presence of the Japanese was not reported until 0830 on 23rd Jan-

The second line of defence on the peninsula

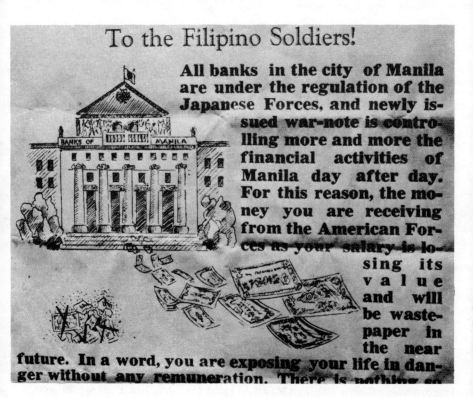

To the Filipino Soldiers!

All banks in the city of Manila are under the regulation of the Japanese Forces, and newly issued war-note is controlling more and more the financial activities of Manila day after day. For this reason, the money you are receiving from the American Forces as your salary is losing its value and will be wastepaper in the near future. In a word, you are exposing your life in danger without any remuneration. There is nothing so

Opposite and above: **Japanese attempts to get the US and Filipino defenders to surrender**

uary. A group some 300 strong had by this time begun moving inland from Longoskawayan Point toward Mount Pucot and were approaching a point at which Bridget had some of his forces. These set out at once to meet the Japanese.

For the latter this first encounter with Bridget's ochoeus warriors was one more macabre experience in a night which had been fraught with such experiences. One wrote in his diary that he had encountered a new American suicide squad dressed in bright yellow uniforms. Whenever they reached an open space they would try to draw Japanese fire 'by sitting down, talking loudly and lighting cigarettes'. All the same, the force showed itself to be more than a match for the Japanese and succeeded not only in clearing them from Mount

Pucot, but also in pushing them back to Longoskawayan Point. Here, however, they were so well entrenched that it soon became obvious that far stronger forces would be needed to dislodge them.

At Quinauan Point the story was somewhat similar and here too local forces contained the invaders.

The story was not yet finished though.

On the night of 26th January an attempt was made to reinforce the troops at Quinauan Point by sending further amphibious landing forces, but these again mistook the landing point and came ashore 200 yards short of the objective at Anyasan Point, where they were easily contained.

Then on 1st February a third force was sent out in a yet bigger and more desperate attempt to exploit the Quinauan beachhead. Homma had himself ordered that this force should be augmented and was to push southeastwards towards Mariveles.

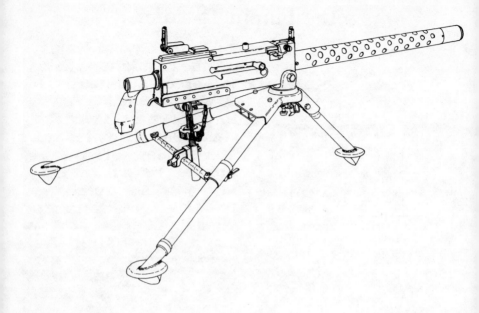

The Browning Caliber .30-inch M1919A4 Light Machine Gun. *Calibre:* .30-inch.
System of operation: recoil automatic. *Overall length:* 41 inches. *Barrel length:*
24 inches. *Feed:* 250-round fabric or disintegrating link belt. *Weight:* 31 lbs (gun)
and 14 lbs (M2 mount). *Muzzle velocity:* 2,800 feet per second. *Cyclic rate of fire:*
400-550 rounds per minute. *Weight of bullet:* 150 grains

A Philippine Army patrol had, however discovered a duplicated order on
the body of a Japanese officer in which
details of the reinforcement attempt
were revealed. As the invaders sailed,
in bright moonlight, the defenders,
thus forewarned, had no difficulty in
spotting them. The Japanese came
under attack from the four remaining
P-40s and, as they approached the
coast, shore-based artillery added to
the havoc.

Then an American patrol joined the
fray. In the end the Japanese invasion
flotilla turned tail and withdrew. The
delighted defenders believed that the
Japanese were returning to Moron.
Actually, unable to make the journey
with many of the boats crippled, the
commander put in at Anyasan Point
where they came ashore unopposed

and were able to complement the
forces already there.

Although the landings had posed no
real threat and called for no increase
in the forces on the spot, it was not
until 8th February, when the Naval
Battalion followed the Japanese
example and themselves adopted the
tactic of amphibious landing behind
the lines, that the invaders were
finally wiped out. Only thirty-four of
the initial landing force succeeded in
escaping in landing barges which
were sent to evacuate the whole force.

Without posing any real threat the
landings at Longoskawayan Point
and Quinauan Point had led to heavy
casualties among the Japanese. 300
men had been killed at Longoskawayan and another 600 at Quinauan. The
2nd Battalion, 20th Infantry, had ceas-

ed to exist as a force.

American losses had also been heavy, however, in the face of suicidal Japanese resistance. Something like 500 men had fallen in the action. As the American Official History puts it: 'It was a heavy price to pay for the security of the West Road.' Nor was this all, for the small unit at Anyasan Point had been built up and it was not to be shifted easily.

Further north, where the main battle was raging, I and II Corps were now ranged along the new line running from Orion to Bagac, with the 2,000-foot high Mount Samat as its commanding centre. Though I Corps still comprised three divisions and II Corps four, both had been badly depleted by the earlier fighting. Nevertheless, the men remained in good spirits.

During the closing days of January Nara instigated several attacks against the new line. These were directed against the Mount Samat positions as it was here that he expected to find the main opposition – men of the 65th Brigade who had assembled in a bamboo thicket had dug trenches almost to the wire of the resistance line. A heavy artillery barrage was laid down and at dusk, following the usual Japanese practice, the attack began.

Once more, however, the Japanese were betrayed by poor Intelligence: they exactly reversed their earlier mistake and attacked the main defensive line of 41st Philippine Division under the impression it was an outpost line. Immediately they came under heavy and punitive machine-gun fire and were forced to call off the attack. The next morning when a count was taken about a hundred Japanese bodies were found, some of them only a few yards from the Filipino foxholes. The defenders suffered only light casualties.

Nara, though discouraged by this failure, persisted and another attack was opened at 1700 on 31st January. Once again there was a heavy artillery barrage, against II Corps' artillery itself and against the lines. As the Japanese shelling stopped, however, II Corps' guns opened up while advanced machine-gunners fired on the assembling Japanese. In a short time plans for the offensive that night were abandoned.

Meanwhile, the Japanese troops, still in the bamboo thickets after the previous night's abortive assault, began to withdraw. The movement was slow because of the large number of wounded and it was two days before it was completed.

To add to Nara's anxieties he was receiving reports from his Intelligence of troop movements behind the American lines. For once the reports were accurate. The units opposite the bamboo thickets were about to launch a counterattack. When it came the attackers encountered fierce opposition from the Japanese still there, and by nightfall on 2nd February had to dig in for the night expecting to have to fight a stiff battle on the morrow. Instead they found the thicket empty of the enemy: the last of the Japs had withdrawn.

Nara was still unwilling to admit defeat. In the next few days there was little more than patrol activity, but by 8th February he was prepared to resume the offensive. That afternoon he told unit commanders to stand by for orders.

But in the meantime Homma, too, had been counting the cost of the battle of Bataan, now five weeks old. That afternoon he telephoned Nara and ordered him to suspend the attack.

Though they did not know it then, the first round of the battle had gone to the defenders. The ragged Filipinos, untrained and unused to war, in their coconut hats, blue denims and rope soled shoes, and the no less ragged Americans, hungry and battle-fatigued – the 'battling bastards of Bataan', as a current song had it – had held the Japanese.

The Breathing Space

If there was now a temporary and uncertain hiatus in the Japanese offensive USAFFE still had plenty to worry them. On the military front although enemy activity was largely reduced to patrol skirmishes, they had in their early attacks on the Orion-Bagac line made several penetrations which had been sealed off, but not without leaving pockets of resistance. The first of these had come into being on 28/29th January when the Japanese had pushed through in the centre of II Corps' sector and created what came to be called the 'Big Pocket'. In its confines were most of the 1,000 men of the 20th Infantry Regiment. Philippine Scouts were at once sent in to attack, but found the enemy too well dug in to be moved. At about the same time a smaller enclave had been set up in I Corps' sector, about half a mile north-west. Then on 6th February, while General Jones was planning to isolate and ring the pockets Lieutenant-General Susumu Morioka opened an offensive which, though halted, caused a deep, narrow salient, regarded as a third pocket.

The Americans and Filipinos began flushing the pockets out, unaware that Morioka had actually ordered a withdrawal, but it was not until about noon on 15th February, that 377 men of the 20th Infantry, all that were left managed to reach the 9th Infantry lines and safety. The withdrawal, covering a matter of yards, had taken four days and during much of the time the Japanese troops had lacked water and food and had subsisted on horseflesh and tree sap.

Of more pressing concern, to the defenders, however than this sporadic fighting was their own food and medical position. This was daily becoming more serious with transport shortages adding to the other difficulties, so that in some parts of the front it proved quite impossible to keep the men supplied during combat. Many had to keep hunger and thirst at bay by chewing on sticks of sugar cane which they cut down where they found them.

The improvised slaughter-houses in southern Bataan were butchering the only available meat, mostly carabao, a sort of indigenous buffalo used by the Filipino farmers as work-horses. This meat was issued to the men every third day and was sometimes augmented or varied by a little fish.

Men had also taken to hunting and fishing and as the campaign wore on began to adopt the eating habits of the Filipinos which had earlier appalled them. They devoured dog meat and even monkey which one gourmet declared was 'all right until the animal's hands turn up on a plate'.

The Filipinos showed no small skill in living off the land and found in the jungles chicken, wild pig, bamboo shoots, mangoes and bananas, while they also ate, with apparent relish, the 'chicken-like' meat of the iguana

A Japanese patrol passes through a Filipino village

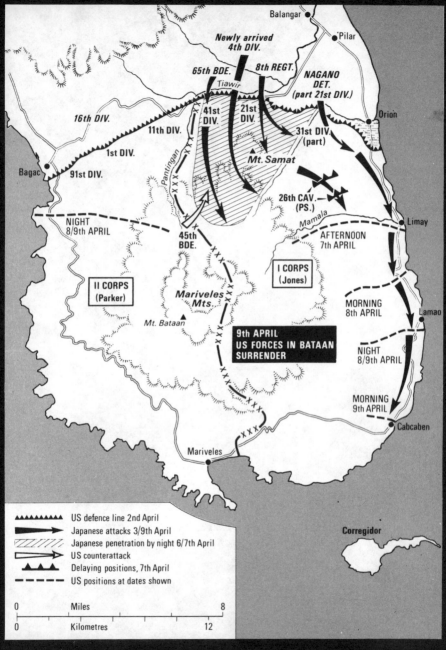

Balangar

Pilar

Newly arrived 4th DIV.

65th BDE.   *8th REGT.*

Tiawir

NAGANO DET. (part 21st DIV.)

Orion

16th DIV.

11th DIV.

1st DIV.

41st DIV.

21st DIV.

31st DIV. (part)

Bagac

91st DIV.

Pantingan

Mt. Samat ▲

26th CAV. (PS.)

Mamala

Limay

NIGHT 8/9th APRIL

45th BDE.

AFTERNOON 7th APRIL

II CORPS (Parker)

Mariveles Mts.

I CORPS (Jones)

MORNING 8th APRIL

Mt. Bataan ▲

Lamao

9th APRIL US FORCES IN BATAAN SURRENDER

NIGHT 8/9th APRIL

MORNING 9th APRIL

Cabcaben

Mariveles

Corregidor

▲▲▲▲▲▲▲▲▲	US defence line 2nd April
➡	Japanese attacks 3/9th April
▨➡	Japanese penetration by night 6/7th April
⇨	US counterattack
▲▲▲	Delaying positions, 7th April
– – –	US positions at dates shown

0	Miles	8
0	Kilometres	12

Resistance on Bataan collapses

lizard and python's eggs. They became skilful at threshing and grinding rice in their foxholes.

A shortage of cigarettes had led to a rampant black market with the price rising daily. Uniforms became threadbare and unrecognisable and great originality was shown in patching and replacing them.

The main concern, however, was disease. Undernourishment meant the men had little resistance to sickness. Because of the speed of the evacuation to Bataan there were few mosquito nets and those there were, were of a heavy and unmanageable type, while quinine to combat and prevent malaria was running dangerously low.

Besides all this, MacArthur had problems of his own. When he first arrived in Corregidor he had set up his headquarters in a barracks on the plateau of 'Topside', the hill which forms one end of the island. From its roof MacArthur stood visible to all watching the Japanese raiders. This was one of his few concessions to the principle enunciated by General Sir Harold Alexander that a commander 'should ensure his troops shall see him'.

When Japanese destruction made the use of this exposed headquarters impossible MacArthur moved into Malinta Tunnel. Originally cut into 'Topside' as a tram-terminal, Malinta's main tunnel had now had a number of laterals driven off from it providing offices, barracks and hospital, as well as USAFFE headquarters and offices for Quezon's government-in-exile. MacArthur's new home accordingly brought him into daily contact with Quezon and his deputy, Osmeña.

Quezon had failed to draw from the war a fundamental lesson: that a country aspiring to political independence cannot expect others to defend it. Under 'War Plan Rainbow V' – the plan now in operation – in the event of America being involved in a war in both Europe and Asia, the European war was to be won first.

Though Quezon had advocated freedom from the yoke of America for decades – including the removal of American bases – he saw this as nothing less than desertion.

And so MacArthur, besides the very solid bombardment of the Japanese, was also subjected to a bombardment of complaint from Quezon – most of it intended for re-direction to Washington – about America's failure to come to the aid of the Philippines. In florid and doom-laden language Quezon spoke of his country 'standing before the Bar of History'. God only knew, he told his people, 'if this is the last time that my voice will be heard before going to my grave'.

Quezon's distress was real, sincere and easy to sympathise with, but much of the chagrin it evoked was used by MacArthur for other purposes. A commander can hardly feel anything but bitter frustration when he realises that the theatre for which he is responsible is taking second place to another. In this situation Quezon was an ally and supporter in bringing weight to bear on Washington.

As the campaign wore on and the Japanese air and artillery attacks brought war to Corregidor itself, Quezon became ever more importunate. MacArthur in his *Reminiscences* speaks of him 'in his wheelchair and racked by tuberculosis'. He told one of MacArthur's staff officers that America 'writhes in anguish at the fate of a distant cousin, Europe, while a daughter, the Philippines, is being raped in the back room'.

The situation came to a head when on 8th February Quezon sent Roosevelt what was virtually an ultimatum in an effort to persuade the American General Staff to send supplies and reinforcements to the island. This was no less than a proposal that the Philippines should be declared independent, forthwith proclaim its neutrality and disband its armed forces. Quezon indicated – and seemed to believe–that under such circumstances the Japanese would remove their

forces.

The message, which had the qualified support of the American High
Commissioner, Sayre, created precisely the sort of shock in Washington
that Quezon no doubt intended.

Roosevelt sent a reply authorising
negotiations for the surrender of the
Filipino troops, but ordering Mac-
Arthur to continue resistance with
his American forces. Privately, the
American president had recorded his
dismay at the total unreality of
Quezon's supposition that the Japanese would respect any declaration
of neutrality and at his blindness to
the 'well known characteristics of the
Japanese towards conquered people'.
But Quezon's threat to declare the
islands neutral can scarcely ever have
been   more   than   a   threat. He,
more than Roosevelt, separated by an
ocean from the harsh reality of com-

**Melinta Tunnel on Corregidor; the last
US bastion in the Philippines**

bat against the Japs, knew how they behaved towards their conquered, for mutilated and tortured American and Filipino bodies had been found on several occasions.

Though he claims, not altogether convincingly, that he could not endorse Quezon's proposals, the letter to Roosevelt probably had the support of MacArthur, particularly since he took the opportunity to enclose a despatch to Marshall in which he said that his forces were 'near done' and that their 'complete destruction' might come at any time.

When it actually came to the point, of course, MacArthur certainly had no intention of surrendering his Filipino troops — further proof the whole action was a bluff. The fact was that MacArthur's and Quezon's crude attempts to force Washington to send relief showed their complete lack of understanding of the supply problems

The defenders of Bataan prepare to resist new Japanese landings

involved. The general had already accused Hart of 'defeatism' because of his unwillingness to hazard his small and vulnerable Asiatic Fleet against the overwhelming sea and air strength of Japan. In Washington there must have been some doubt on another score: whether, in view of experience so far, whatever help was sent would be put to any better use. The 'biggest concentration of heavy bombers anywhere in the world' had been lost on the first day of the war and the Japanese had obtained virtual tactical surprise when they landed at precisely those points MacArthur had claimed to have forecast they would land, and with forces infinitely smaller than his own.

Equally, both he and Quezon took the priorities of 'Rainbow' far too literally. Putting the European war first had never been intended to mean they were to be entirely deprived of assistance. Efforts to put into operation a blockade-running service to Luzon from Australia were fraught

Above: Osmena, Quezon's vice-president. *Below:* during the defence of the peninsula, Quezon went over MacArthur's head to attempt to obtain more troops

with difficulties, even before the Japanese overran the Dutch East Indies in late February. There were few vessels of sufficient size and speed in Australia, crews were in short supply and those which could be found needed hefty premiums to tempt them to such risks.

None of this meant, however, that the American supply officers carrying out Marshall's instructions in Darwin were failing to try, or to seek alternative means if the sea-routes proved impossible. Two methods which had been examined were by means of submarines and by air freight, but it had to be recognised that neither of these could bring anything but small scale relief.

At the time of Quezon's letter to Roosevelt all this activity going on in Darwin was unknown, either to the defenders of Bataan or to the government and military command on Corregidor, and there is no doubt that the apparent failure to supply them was causing considerable problems and increasing the sense of being deserted among the men.

From this the Japanese were making propaganda capital. Their radio station, KZRH Manila, was using the theme song 'The Ships that Never Came', while its seductive-voiced women announcers played programmes of popular songs calculated to make the Americans feel homesick.

Upon the Filipino themselves they tried other means. One of these was the offer of speedy independence. The ageing General Aguinaldo, the freedom leader against whom MacArthur's father had fought, was brought to the microphone to urge that resistance should cease, reminding his listeners that the Japanese had promised prompt 'independence with honour'. The Japanese Prime Minister, Tojo, had made a promise to this effect in the Diet, he said.

An appeal of such a nature and from such a source must seem to lend support to Quezon's own plan and Washington was deeply disturbed by it.

On 20th February, Quezon, ostensibly in the interests of his own safety, was taken by submarine with his wife Doña Aurora and his vice-president, Osmeña, to Australia. His departure was marked by a characteristically dramatic gesture. As MacArthur went to see him off he slipped the signet ring from his own finger and put it on the general's. 'When they find your body,' he said, 'I want them to know you fought for my country.'

With Quezon safely under the eyes of the US government in America the war could be prosecuted without risk of political embarrassment.

Despite the last ditch 'fight to destruction' he described to Marshall and Quezon's parting words, MacArthur had not yet given up hope. It had been suggested that his wife, Jean and his son, Arthur, should depart on the same submarine as Quezon, but this his wife had stoically refused to consider. The next day, 21st February, there came intimation from Marshall that Washington had its own views about MacArthur's

High ranking Japanese officers arrive in captured Manila

future. This had been under consideration for some time and it was generally felt that it would be wrong to sacrifice him. He was now therefore, told that he would be required to move his headquarters to Mindanao in the extreme south of the Philippines and then to go to Australia, there to take command of the Allied Forces in the south-west Pacific.

MacArthur said that his first reaction was to ignore the order and he even threatened to resign his commission and join the Bataan defence forces as a volunteer. Such a gesture was, as he well knew, an empty one and there were, furthermore, plenty of people round him to persuade him that his best course was to go to Australia to lead the forces which would return and liberate the archepelago.

There were, nevertheless, many reasons why MacArthur was reluctant to leave. One was that with the departure of Quezon, he felt that the responsibilities of government – which in practice had rested on him ever since the beginning of hostilities – were now his in fact, in addition to his command of the armies.

Equally strong was the feeling that a turning point in the battle had been reached. An army which has known nothing but a succession of defeats, however honourable these may be, is likely to magnify any apparent success. The Japanese abandonment of their offensive undoubtedly appeared to the embattled defenders of Bataan as a notable victory. Indeed, there were officers advocating that they should now break out of the peninsula. (Homma was later to admit that had an offensive been launched his forces would have been in no condition to meet it.) MacArthur, however, was too much of a realist to see that without air superiority this was an idle hope – it is one thing to recapture lost ground and quite another to hold it.

All the same, he was sufficiently imbued with the euphoria of the time to plan offensives which would take Olongapo and with it the Japanese supply base at Subic Bay, which he believed if snatched in a quick *coup* would solve his own supply problems.

Also indicative of the minds of the defenders and their commander was the fact that on 8th March his communiqué quoted a rumour that Homma unable to bear the ignominy of defeat, had committed *hara-kiri*. The rumour was completely untrue, though after the manner of such apocrypha it was embellished with much 'substantiating' incidental detail (Homma in a strange tribute to his enemy, was said to have immolated himself in MacArthur's old apartments at the Manila Hotel!)

At the same time he may also have learned that the three relief ships had been chartered and set sail from Darwin. Everything seemed to indicate that a change was about to take place in the defenders, fortunes and it was probably the combination of these factors which led MacArthur to seek to delay his departure. He told Marshall on 25th February that he would go to Mindanao about 15th March.

Homma, when he saw the reports of his death, must have gained from them some wry amusement, but, though he was still very much alive, Imperial Headquarters were far from pleased with him. They had never placed great importance on the Philippines which, since they possessed no raw materials the Japanese required, had been seen by them only as a strategic barrier to their ambitions elsewhere and as a springboard for the other' attacks. Witness to this was their readiness to deprive Homma of some of his best troops at the height of his campaign, and it was the loss of these, as much as the efforts of the defenders, which had led to the abandonment of the offensive.

However, inspecting officers sent from Army High Command in Tokyo were not at all pleased to find Japanese officers living in style in Manila while the battle of Bataan was at its height and as a result a number of staff officers including Homma's Chief of Staff, Lieutenant-General Masami Maeda, were transferred.

The inspecting officers recognised all the same that the American forces in the Philippines had been underestimated both in numbers and in will to resist and in the middle of March reinforcements began to arrive. Nara's 65th Brigade and the 16th Division each received 3,500 men and on 15th March Lieutenant-General Kenzo Kitano's 4th Division arrived from Shanghai. There was no enthusiasm for these reinforcements among Fourteenth Army Staff. The 4th Division Homma regarded as the 'worst equipped division in the whole Japanese army'. It consisted of 11,000 men.

Artillery, including heavy guns, had been arriving for some time and ten of these, 240mm howitzers, the most powerful pieces the Japanese possessed, had been emplaced to bombard Corregidor and its offshore islands, Fort Frank and Fort Drum. They added greatly to the discomfort of life and caused considerable damage to Fort Frank.

Little harm came to Fort Drum, however. It had been christened by the men USS Drum, as the reef of rocks on which it stood had been entirely encased in concrete making it look like a stationary battleship, and against this the bursting shells, though they chipped away chunks up to four inches thick, made little impact.

In the second week of March a submarine was to be sent to convey MacArthur with his family to Mindanao, on the first stage of their journey to Australia. There had, however, now been no action on the battle front for three weeks and MacArthur decided that instead of waiting for the submarine's arrival he would leave three days earlier, travelling by motor torpedo boat.

Before he left he called for General Wainwright, whom he appointed commander of the forces in his absence, instructing him to 'hold on' until he got back and bequeathing him his plan for the attack on Olongapo. There was little doubt that at this time MacArthur had convinced himself he was going to Australia merely to summon the relieving forces which, under his own dynamic leadership, would run the Japanese gauntlet.

In the evening, he embarked with Jean, their small son and Ah Cheu, their Chinese nurse, at South Dock. MacArthur took with him Sutherland and other members of his own staff, as well as senior signals, engineer, antiaircraft and air officers.

At 2115 hours the convoy of four boats sailed. They successfully evaded the enemy blockade and on Friday, 14th March reached Cagayan in Mindanao.

Four B-17s had gone from Australia to meet the party, but only one arrived and this was so decrepit it was sent back empty. A further three were ordered and on 16th March two arrived and the party took off arriving at Batchelor Field, Darwin, at 0900 on the 17th.

Shortly after landing MacArthur held a press conference. There he told reporters that he believed he had been sent to Australia to organise an offensive, one of the main intentions of which was the liberation of the Philippines.

'I came through,' he told them, in his famous dramatic lines, 'and I shall return.'

Soon after Major-General George H Brett, commander of the American forces in Australia, telephoned John Curtin, the Australia Prime Minister, to tell him officially that MacArthur had arrived to take command.

He suggested that it would be a gesture 'highly acceptable' to the President and 'pleasing to the American people', if MacArthur was nominated by the Australian government as Supreme Commander of all Allied forces in the south-west Pacific. Curtin had no difficulty in persuading his own Cabinet and that day Washington and London were told of the arrangement.

Bataan: The Final Round

For an army, besieged, hungry, disease-ridden, fighting a desperate defensive action, the departure of the official rulers of the country it is defending, followed by that of its own commander-in-chief, would normally seem like the ultimate acts of desertion, the final acceptance of the hopelessness of the situation. That it did not have that effect in this case was due to two things: the defenders' conviction that they had inflicted a telling defeat on the enemy and the belief – which he himself shared – that

MacArthur had gone simply to ginger up and collect the relieving forces.

His departure seemed, therefore, rather to offer hope than discouragement.

Among Wainwright's first actions when he took over command was to rename USAFFE as USFIP – United States Forces in the Philippines, and to appoint Brigadier-General Edward King, USAFFE artillery officer, to his own now-vacant command of the Luzon Force. King became, under this arrangement, Wainwright's represen-tative in Bataan, but neither he nor his superior had any delusions about the difficulty of carrying out Mac-Arthur's order to 'hold on'.

The Orion-Bagac line, like its predecessor further north, was divided between I and II Corps and was thir-teen miles long. General Jones was now in charge of Wainwright's old I Corps sector. He had under command some 32,000 men, while Parker's II

Captured US forces are marched out of Bataan

Japanese engineers back up the drive on Bataan

Corps on the right or eastward side, had 28,000. The principal remaining infantry force, the Philippine Division was in Luzon Force Reserve.

I Corps had some fifty artillery pieces, mostly 75mm calibre and, with only two howitzers. II Corps had about 100 guns, again predominantly 75mms, but with thirty-one naval guns, up to 3-inch calibre, and twelve mountain guns. The main difficulties were lack of air observation, howitzers, fire control, communications equipment and motor transport.

Nevertheless, considerable defensive preparation had been made during the lull in Homma's offensive. Troops had been trained in jungle warfare, the defence line had been improved, and trenches and dugouts replaced the foxholes of the earlier stages of the battle. Mines had been laid and the whole front had been screened by a twelve foot palisade of bamboo. This, while of little value as an obstruction, gave the troops a feeling of security and enabled them to carry out their tasks without constant enemy scrutiny.

To most of the defenders, however, the main enemy had ceased to be the Japanese; food and disease, in their combined and endless onslaught, were wreaking a far more terrible havoc. The five gramme preventive doses of quinine the men had been given against malaria ran out in the first week of March, and since then the number of cases had risen enormously. Soon thirty-five per cent of front line units were affected. By the middle of March there were 3,000 men in hospital, by the end of March 4,000 new cases a day and it was estimated that seventy-five to eighty per cent of front line troops were sick.

It was about this time that three of the vessels which had been organised to run the Japanese blockade reached Cebu in the Visayas. They brought with them 10,000 tons of food and 4,000,000 rounds of ammunition. To try to help fight sickness medical supplies were sent air freight. All this, however, brought little relief to the men on Bataan as no way was found of transporting the supplies from Cebu to the places where they were needed.

In mid-March, too, Filipino and American army patrols encountered increased opposition and realised that the Japanese would not be long in renewing their offensive. Homma had been making his plans for some time past as the reinforcements began to arrive, but the truth was that he was not having an easy time either. Battle casualties, disease and malnutrition had their effects on his efficiency and had reduced his infantry strength considerably. It was proving difficult to keep the Fourteenth Army supplied and rations had been cut from sixty-two ounces to twenty-three. His men, too, were prey to malaria and other tropical diseases and between 1st January and 31st March 13,000 men were in hospital. It was this, among other factors, which had led to the abandonment of his first offensive.

While the reinforcements which had arrived were by no means what Homma had asked for, the situation now looked better. There was heavy artillery, two air force heavy bombardment regiments comprising sixty twin-engined bombers, as well as some naval air force units.

Accordingly he made his plans. The centre of the defence line was dominated by Mount Samat which gave good observation across the Japanese and on whose slopes the Americans had emplaced much of their artillery. Homma saw that he must take the mountain and planned to do this in a movement which would carry his forces south-eastward towards Limay, ringing the mountains to turn westwards towards Mariveles. The plan was completed and issued to commanders on 20th March. At the same time he was not going to allow an opportunity to the defenders to re-group on Corre-

Brigadier-General King

gidor and preparation for an attack on the island-fortress was begun right away.

The attack on Samat was to be made by the newly arrived 4th Division, supported by Nara's 65th Brigade, while a detachment of the 21st Division, some 4,000 strong, under Major-General Kameichiro Nagano, which had arrived in late February was to cover the eastern flank of this attacking force. At the same time the 16th Division would make a feint attack on I Corps' front. The combined air forces were to launch heavy attacks on the American lines and just before the infantry assault there would be an intensive artillery bombardment. D-Day was set for 3rd April and zero-hour, after some argument, was to be 1500 hours.

Before committing his men to this offensive Homma tried one last appeal to Wainwright, whom he now knew to have succeeded MacArthur. In notes, packed in beer cans with ribbons attached, and dropped from aircraft, he commanded Wainwright to accept the reality of 'honourable defeat'. The appeal was, of course, ignored, but about 24th March a Filipino patrol found, among documents on a dead Japanese officer, orders for a reconnaissance in force on Mount Samat

Left: the modern 'knights of bushido' are triumphant. Above: an American commander discusses surrender terms after the Japanese breakthrough. Below: Japanese gunners in action on Bataan

which was to be the preliminary to an attack on the mountain sometime after 26th March. Defensive preparations in the area were redoubled, and shortly afterwards the Japanese began their air assualt which was to be the offensive's first phase. There were now so few anti-aircraft guns left that the planes could bomb and strafe at will.

Good Friday 1942 fell on 3rd April, a date which also held significance for the Japanese as the anniversary of the death of Emperor Jimmu, according to legend the first occupant of the Imperial throne. They were determined that their attacks started on so propitious a day should be brought to a successful conclusion before another anniversary – 29th April, which was Emperor Hirohito's birthday.

The day was hot and dry. In the early morning American observers on Samat saw the Japs preparing their guns to fire. They counted some nineteen batteries of artillery and about ten mortar batteries. At about 0900 the barrage began with almost 150 guns firing in the biggest bombardment of the campaign. As it was going on aircraft were also raiding the front line positions. Defences carefully prepared over the past weeks were churned up, telephone line knocked down, canebreaks and fields concealing troops and weapons set ablaze.

The artillery and aerial bombardment lasted until the afternoon and then the infantry assault began. Nara's 65th Brigade tanks pierced the line on the left of II Corps and continued to progress southwards crossing the Tiawar River where the Filipino defenders broke after brief resistance. By nightfall the Japanese smilingly told each other that their offensive had succeeded beyond all hopes. Tired, sick, hungry, the defenders in many cases had their spirit of resistance broken by the preliminary bombardment before the attack proper began. At least one unit, the 41st Division,

US and Filipino forces surrender to the Japanese on Bataan

Philippine Army, had virtually ceased to exist as a military unit after the remorseless shelling. The success was such that the normally cautious Homma abandoned all restraint and ordered his troops to go on and take Mount Samat on the 4th.

Late in the afternoon Parker was forced to release his only reserves to try to fill the gaping breaches which had been driven into his line.

The following day, the Saturday of Holy Week, began, as Good Friday had begun, with a massive artillery bombardment. Some Filipino units pulled out of line before the ground assault started. Nara's troops cut round the flank of the remaining defenders in his sector and they had to be hurriedly withdrawn to avert envelopment.

At the same time the 4th Division, of which so little had been expected, was pushing forward successfully. An armoured thrust gained control of the Pilar-Bagac Road. The 21st Division, Philippine Army, fell back in disorder. The same day the 8th Infantry Regiment, entering battle for the first time, broke the Philippine lines at another point. Just after 1000 hours the defenders had withdrawn from the whole of the main line of resistance.

The Japanese had good reason for self-congratulation. All this had happened in the preliminary sorties – the main attack was not scheduled till noon! By the end of the day they were twenty-four hours ahead of schedule and they were now in a position to storm Mount Samat.

In the fastness of the Bataan jungle the Americans and Filipinos were gathering for Easter Sunday services when the Japanese bombardment began once more. At 1000 two columns of the 4th Division moved out, but ran into stubborn resistance from the 21st Division, now in a new resistance line and made little initial progress. However, a breakthrough on their left allowed the Japanese to get behind the artillery and the gunners had to destroy their weapons and pull hurriedly to the rear.

For the rest of the day it was a story of continual Japanese advance with the defenders reaching a new line, regrouping and then being forced back as it became untenable. In the late afternoon the speed of the advance was such that the 21st Division's command post was overrun. The staff managed to escape along the trails, but the divisional commander, Brigadier-General Mateo Capinpin, was captured. Half an hour later the remaining artillery of the 21st Division came under attack. The gunners had to flee, this time without even the opportunity to destroy their guns.

That night the two advancing Japanese columns met at the now-evacuated 21st Division command post.

By Easter Monday the overriding intention of the defenders was to hold the advance long enough to be able to mount a counterattack. All available troops were moved from the reserve for this purpose. They included even men of the 803rd Engineer Battalion, US Army, who were ordered to cease all engineering activity and prepare for combat. However, as these forces began to move towards the line for the planned counterattack which was to try to clear the slopes of Mount Samat of the Japanese, they found the roads blocked by retreating Filipino troops, making movement almost impossible.

By the time they reached the line, the disintegration of the 21st Division had deprived them of their jumping-off points. New ones were hastily designated, but possession even of these was contested. The 21st itself, which was to have taken part in the counterattack, was now reduced to 800 men. Then, while its commander was seeking instruction, the Japanese attacked the 31st Infantry outposts nearby and the force sent to swing the pendulum from defensive to offensive was itself forced into a defensive role.

It was the same up and down the line. In one place the 41st Infantry made small gains, but a Japanese counterattack followed and they were driven back to the Pantigan River. The 45th Infantry Regiment advanced just over a mile, pushing back some 65th Brigade outposts, and were then held by a strong Japanese defence line where they dug in, believing the counterattack was to be continued in the morning. There was no such intention. It was being acknowledged that the counterattack had been a failure.

The defenders' situation was now desperate. The left half of II Corps line had been driven in and the two corps were now split and incapable of mutual assistance. Mount Samat was occupied and the Japanese were threatening to turn II Corps' flank and push it eastwards to the sea. They had advanced some 7,000 yards beyond the main line of resistance.

Catastrophe faced the defenders of Bataan. Frantic efforts were made to reform lines, but they had to be abandoned before they were occupied as the Japanese pressed relentlessly forward. Orders were issued and had to be revoked because they were impossible of execution as the defending army poured to the rear in such numbers roads were jammed.

As the break up of the armies continued units disappeared and were never heard of again. 'In two days,' remarks the US Official History, 'an army evaporated into thin air.'

And all the time the Japanese were pushing down the east coast. The 26th Cavalry, which had already fought with such distinction, was called upon once again to try to remedy the situation, but now the famous Scout regiment was without horses – slaughtered because of lack of forage. They attacked the Japanese 8th Infantry Regiment nonetheless. Incapable of defeating the foe in frontal attack they tried an outflanking movement whereupon the Japanese artillery opened up with all its force and the troops were attacked by planes of the 16th Light Bombardment Regiment, with such heavy casualties that the Scouts were pulled back across the

An American warehouse burns on Cebu

Mamala River.

Wainwright, reporting to Washington, could tell of nothing but retreat. By the night of 7th April, the Japs had almost won an offensive they expected to last nearly a month. The entire main line of resistance of II Corps was taken. A line along the Mamala River had to be evacuated.

All this had been done at a cost of some 630 Japanese casualties. One unit had had no battle casualties at all

Now Wainwright turned his attention to the contingency plan MacArthur had left him: the seizure of Olongapo. If this failed the troops involved would try to escape to the forests and join the guerilla forces already fighting there.

Even as he issued the orders he knew the emptiness of this last hope. The sick and half-starved men were at the end of resistance. General Jones, whose I Corps was to carry out the attack, had no option but to say it was impossible.

In fact, on Bataan, things were far worse than Wainwright knew. So much worse that his representative on the spot, King, had come to a decision of his own. An intelligent and highly qualified officer, he had a law degree and had studied at both command and staff schools. Liked by officers and men, this quietly-spoken, courteous man had reached the painful conclusion that there remained no course but surrender. Knowing this would be completely counter to Wainwright's order and wanting to spare him the responsibility he sent emissaries forward under flag of truce without informing his commander.

It was not until 0600 that day, 9th April, that Wainwright learnt of King's action. Bitterly disappointed he begged for reconsideration. But it was now too late. At 0900 King, dressed in his last clean uniform, went forward to meet the commander of Japanese 21st Division, General Nagano.

The meeting took place at an experimental farm station near the lines. Nagano at once told them that he was not himself authorised to make arrangements, but that Homma had been told and that a representative of Fourteenth Army was due at any moment. A few minutes later the chief of operations, Colonel Motu Nagayama arrived.

Nagayama declared he would negotiate with no one but Wainwright and refused to accept King's statement that he could surrender only the troops under his own command and not all troops in the Philippines. He equally rejected King's request for an immediate armistice and a cessation of all air bombardment. He refused to listen to repeated pleas that prisoners should be treated in accordance with the provisions of the Geneva Convention and frequently reiterated that the only terms he was prepared to consider were those which included the surrender of all forces. In the end it was agreed that if the troops on Bataan wished to surrender they would have to do so individually and unconditionally. At 1230 King agreed to surrender unconditionally himself in order to save his men. Two of the men in his party, with a Japanese officer, were then sent back to pass on the news and to inform troops on their route.

That day there fell into Japanese hands all but 2,000 of the Bataan Defence Force. Those few managed to shorten their sojourn in the Japanese POW compounds by escaping to Corregidor. Not so some 78,000 of their comrades.

And so, on 9th April, the battle of Bataan ended. It had lasted three months. If Homma's final victory had come more speedily than he had anticipated it had also taken him 123 days to achieve what he set out to do in 50.

Yet for the men who had defended the peninsula the days of agony were not over. The Japanese forced their captives to march from Mariveles to San Fernando, a distance of sixty-five miles. Hungry and thirsty, many of them in the fevers of malaria, with the sun beating down on them, they stumbled along their road. Hundreds were clubbed and beaten to death. A cruel and ignominious end was inflicted by those who claimed to honour the warriors virtues upon those who had shown them.

With the fall of Bataan the scene was almost, but not quite, set for the final act. There were still American and Filipino forces holding out in the southern islands of Mindanao and the Visayas. Though the Japanese in Davao had attempted to extend their foothold, the forces in Mindanao, under Brigadier-General William F Sharp, had held them in check. This had been done with three Filipino divisions and some Philippine Constabulary units, all poorly trained – not all could fire a rifle – and with equipment matching their training: defective machine-guns, no anti-tank weapons, grenades or steel helmets. Their artillery consisted of eight old 3-inch mountain guns, three of which had been lost in Davao.

These forces, with no possibility of reinforcement after the retreat to Bataan, were under orders to defend the 'whole area south of Luzon' and when this ceased to be possible were to break up into small guerilla groups.

In the Visayas were some 20,000 men organised into five garrisons spread throughout the islands and jointly under the command of Brigadier-General Bradford G Chynoweth. They had one major advantage over Sharp's troops: they were backed up by a well-organised resistance movement, already in being, and called *Baus Au* or 'Get it Back'!

Now that the battle for Bataan was over Homma could at last give attention to these defensive outposts and four days before King's surrender some 5,000 men, mostly from the 35th Brigade and the 124th Infantry Regiment, set sail for Cebu Island in the Visayas which they were to seize before moving on to Mindanao. Once that had been taken the other garrisons could be neutralised.

Chynoweth was warned of an approaching attack-convoy of three cruisers and eleven transports on the day of the surrender of Bataan, 9th April. Shortly after dawn one assault force landed at Cebu City while a second landed in the centre of Toledo on the opposite side of the island. By the end of the day the overwhelming

Jap forces had pushed back the defenders and were in undisputed control of Cebu City. Among booty captured were the supplies brought at such risk from Darwin the previous month and never delivered to the men for whom they were intended. Just sufficient time was gained by the defenders for the demolition teams to destroy bridges and approach roads. At Toledo the Japanese were equally successful. Here, only a small force of infantry was holding the defences as it was thought the terrain would prohibit amphibious attack. After resisting stubbornly they had to withdraw leaving the Japanese in possession of Toledo.

This was the last standing defence An attempt to establish a new line miscarried, largely because the demolition teams waited too long and then fled before the advancing Japanese armour. On the night of the 12th Chynoweth and about 200 men made for the mountains to carry out their instructions to wage guerilla war.

On 16th April, Wainwright, having conceded the loss of Cebu Island, ordered General Sharp to re-establish the Visayan-Mindanao Force and take command of the remaining garrisons in the Visayas.

On the same day the enemy began landing on another of the Visayan islands, Panay, where similar defensive arrangements to those at Cebu were in operation. Again they came ashore at two points and two days later a further landing took place. By 20th April the strategic points of the island were in Japanese hands and the battle for Panay was over. Like Chynoweth's forces the defenders under their commander, Colonel Albert F Christie, made for the mountains where the *Baus Au* had collected a cache of supplies of food, ammunition and fuel as well as cattle, and had even established rice-mills. The guerillas were preparing for a long battle. Hit and run raids were started almost immediately and were so effective that the Japanese were forced to mount a punitive expedition. In what was certainly one of the most extraordinary 'irregular' action of the Philippine war, Filipinos armed only with bows and arrows and *bolos* ambushed the Japanese on the mountain trails, killing many, and forcing the rest into hasty retreat.

The action was a mere sideshow, nonetheless. The Japanese were in undisputed control of the two main islands of the Visayas.

Early on the morning of 29th April – the emperor's birthday – the first landings on Mindanao took place at Cotabato and Parang on the west coast. At Cotabato the defenders were forced out of the town and prepared what was planned as an extended stand on the outskirts. This failed because the forces at Parang, after holding firm for more than three hours, finally broke, leaving the main highway to Cotabato open to the Japanese and the defenders there had to pull back. The Japanese continued to advance next day and between 29th April and 3rd May the Japanese force of about 5,000 men gained control of almost all southern Mindanao.

Only in the Cagayan region in the north were the Filipinos able to offer resistance. But that day, 3rd May, a new Japanese landing took place. Sharp was forced to commit his reserves to try to hold the Sayre Highway, one of the main routes of the island, and an attempt was made to counterattack. This came to nothing because of the speed of the Japanese advance and the rest of the story was confusion and retreat interspersed by moments of sacrificial and heroic resistance.

But already, some days before, Homma had decided that the troops in the area could handle the conquest of Mindanao unaided and turned his attention elsewhere: toward Corregidor where Wainwright's continued occupancy was still denying the Japs the use of Manila Bay. This, the the Japanese commander decided, had gone on long enough.

The Impregnable 'Rock'

The troops on Corregidor had an almost superstitious belief in its invulnerability. With its solid defences built in rock, its labyrinthine Malinta Tunnel, and separated as it was from mainland Luzon by a two-mile channel, like a mediaeval castle in its moat, it seemed to defy the strongest enemy.

Even after the destruction of Cavite the men on the island had gone on living a life much the same as in peacetime on the three-and-a-half by one-and-a-half-mile 'Rock'. They paraded in smart, crisp uniforms or played cards and billiards in orderly rooms. Canteens and clubs were open. In the officers' club dance bands played the night away.

To the men of Colonel Samuel Lutz Howard's 4th Marines, when they

Japanese aircraft over Corregidor; the last US stronghold

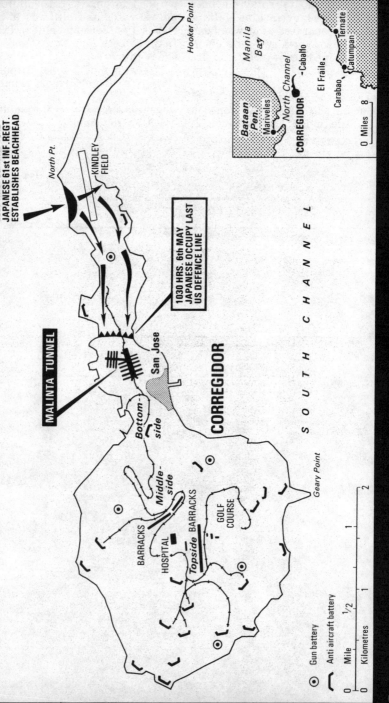

The island fortress of Corregidor falls to 1,000 Japanese troops despite a defending force of 15,000

arrived there from Olongapo, the Rock seemed an unbelievable haven amid the horrors of war. They could not ignore the incessant air raid warnings with the bravado displayed by the island's permanent denizens, but they, too, soon began to accept the legend of its unassailability.

Such was the convinction of its strength that as late as 27th December, when the Japanese were advancing in their pincer-movement through north and south Luzon, Radio Manila was challenging them to bomb the island. When, in their own time, the Japanese accepted the challenge the myth of impregnability received its first blow.

Their air attacks marked the beginning of the drive on the Rock and they were to grow in intensity concurrently with Homma's second offensive against Bataan. The whole campaign was marked by that methodical thoroughness which had characterised all the Japanese onslaughts.

Day after day the planes came back. The anti-aircraft gunners grew more and more accurate, but were still hampered, as everywhere else, by the short range of their guns, and had to wait until the bombers were directly overhead before firing. This meant waiting for the nerve-racking moment when the bombs were actually released. It also meant that as many rounds as possible had to be fired in the short period in which the planes were in range. None the less, the gunners not only succeeded in keeping the planes so high that many strategic points on the island, such as the power station and the water pumping station, were spared, they also accounted for some twenty-five planes. One battery became so proficient that it reached a rate of fire of thirty-four rounds per minute. All this did much to encourage the defenders, though it did little to effect the formidable Jap air forces.

After mid-January the raids ceased, but the island had been left a shambles and, to make matters worse, accommodation designed to take a force of 6,000 men had something like 15,000.

Men from the destroyed Cavite Naval base were there and with them the staffs of USAFFE headquarters and service establishments in Manila, as well as the Philippine Government with its retinues. In these circumstances the bombing raids could scarcely avoid causing havoc and heavy casualties. Furthermore, the added numbers – on top of the fact that it was no longer possible to supply the island – had placed heavy pressure on provisions and much of the men's time was spent in finding the means of subsistence.

The arrival in March of ten of the most powerful artillery pieces of the Japanese Army, the 240mm howitzers of the Ist Heavy Artillery Regiment, added to the torment. Until then the only artillery within range were small calibre guns at Ternate, twelve miles away.

The final assault on Bataan gave the inhabitants of Corregidor and the other islands a short respite as the guns were wanted there. After two days, however, the bombers were back. A force of sixty army and twenty-four naval aircraft flying from Clark Field made three or four sorties a day so the defenders were under air attack for as much as eight hours a day. And then, not content with this daylong bombardment, the Japanese began night attacks in waves of fifty bombers at a time.

Though all this had told on nerves morale was still high. The Japanese had inflicted far fewer casualties than might have been expected, which helped to sustain the illusion that in Corregidor, 'The Rock', 'the Gibraltar of the East', the men were safe. Now they longed for the Japanese to begin their infantry assaults, certain they could repel them. Here, perhaps, they would show the enemy, was one corner of Asia where the Knights of Bushido were not invincible.

When Bataan fell, therefore, they were aware only of an invigorating feeling of being in the front line. Some of the pessimists, it was true, said that

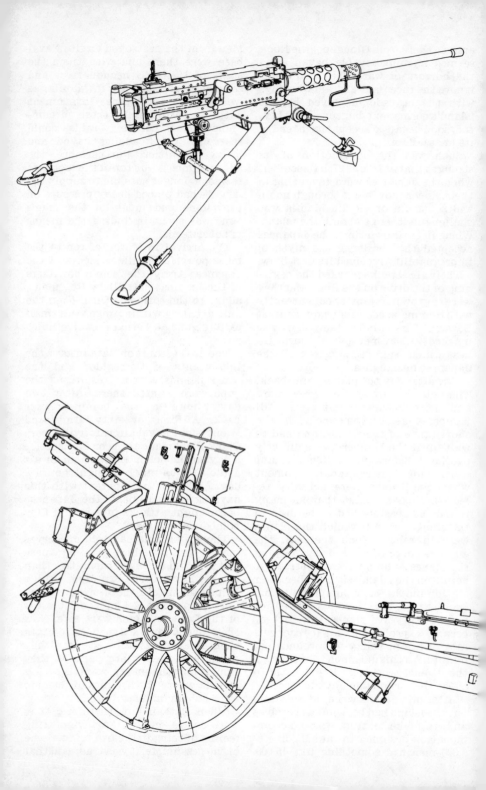

The Browning Caliber .50-inch Heavy Barrel M2 Machine Gun. *Calibre:* .50-inch. *System of operation:* Recoil, selective fire. *Overall length:* 65.1 inches. *Barrel length:* 45 inches. *Feed:* Disintegrating link belt. *Weight:* 84 lbs (gun) and 44½ lbs (M3 tripod mount). *Muzzle velocity:* 2,930 feet per second (firing M2 ball ammunition). *Cyclic rate of fire:* 450-550 rounds per minute. *Weight of Bullet:* 1.71 ounces.

The Japanese Model 91 (1931) 105mm Howitzer. *Calibre:* 105mm. *Weight of shell:* 35 lbs. *Types of shell:* HE, APHE, pointed, shrapnel and incendiary. *Length of barrel:* 24 calibres, 8 feet 4 inches. *Muzzle velocity:* 1,790 feet per second. *Ranges:* 11,772 yards (Charge 1), 8,502 yards (Charge 2), 6,322 (Charge 3) and 5,123 (Charge 4). *Rate of fire:* 6-8 rounds per minute maximum. 2 rounds per minute for 15 minutes and 50-60 rounds per hour continuously. *Elevation:* —5 degrees to + 45 degrees *Traverse:* 40 degrees (20 degrees left and right)

now Bataan had gone the Japanese would be able to bring their artillery to bear on Corregidor from the tip of the peninsula. They were promptly told that the Japs, equally, would now be under fire from Corregidor's guns. The American artillerymen were as good as their word. One battery hit a Japanese artillery concentration with 670lb shells, then destroyed a second battery, an ammunition dump and a

tank park. The greatest disadvantages for the gunners, however, was their lack of air support. Gun-laying had to be done from maps or from observations points on the Rock's highest points.

They now began to understand the difficulties under which they laboured. In the Mariveles area of Bataan, the Japanese had assembled a squadron of observation planes and a balloon company. Besides their 240mm guns, now only three miles away, they had forty-six 15mm guns, twenty-eight 105mm guns and thirty-two 75mms. Safe from the attack Japanese observers in balloons could pick out targets on the Rock and direct the guns.

On 29th April, the ferocity of the artillery bombardment – in honour of the Emperor's birthday – was suddenly increased, indicating to the defenders that the Japanese were soon to attempt their assault on the island. The fire was almost continuous from 0730 and the blast waves from the detonations of the 240mm shells were such that the defenders waiting in their foxholes for the anticipated invasion force were often picked up and thrown down by them. At the same time wave after wave of bombers was passing overhead, but such was the artillery fire that their presence went almost unnoticed by its victims.

By midday the whole island seemed ablaze from end to end. The fires started set off some of the ammunition dumps which had not been hit by shells.

For two days the barrage continued. Throughout the guns seemed to be firing like machine-guns. Then, almost unbelievably, on 2nd May, it actually began to intensify. During the five-hour long bombardment the Japanese fired more than 3,600 rounds, one of which smashed through the concrete covering of an ammunition store so that it went up as if, so the Japanese observers said, the whole island had exploded.

Japanese barges leave Bataan for the assault on Corregidor

Japanese barges leave Bataan for the assault on Corregidor

Men at the far end of the island began having ear and nose haemorrhages from concussion. Thirteen-ton mortars were lifted from their mounts and flew through the air. One was carried 150 yards.

As the guns died down men staggered out and began what had become a daily routine: the task of digging out their comrades.

Homma, however, was still not quite ready for the final assault. Most of his landing craft were up in Lingayen Gulf and sailing them round the coasts and down the channel to the staging areas at Limay meant exposing them to the guns of Corregidor. In the end they had to be brought down under cover of an artillery bombardment.

While they were on their way Homma's men were making bamboo scaling ladders with which to climb the high cliff of the island.

Next morning, 5th May, the Japanese again shelled the Rock with every gun they had. As it continued through the day communications cables were severed, searchlights knocked out, land mines exploded, machine gun posts caved in, wire was cut and the foxholes on the beach flattened out.

At 1830 the concentration of shellfire began to move down the islands towards its elongated tail. At 2130 sound locators picked up the engines of landing craft warming up.

Half an hour earlier Colonel Howard, commander of the 4th Marines, had ordered all weapons to be brought from cover and sent men to the beach defences. The defenders looked more like an insurgent rabble than a collection of regular soldiers. They included not only the marines, Filipino troops and the remains of the Philippine Scouts – all in ragged, dirty and unkempt uniforms – but even civilians

Only a small portion of the Japanese troops destined for Corregidor actually landed

Above: unconcerned US troops relax on the 'Impregnable Rock'
Below: the small Japanese landing parties attack the defenders

Above: a captured P-40 undergoes Japanese inspection on Mindanao.
Below: General Wainwright surrenders the Philippines to General Homma

Left: with the fall of Corregidor the door to the south was open. *Above:* General Wainwright broadcasts the terms of the surrender. *Below:* the victors and the vanquished

who had volunteered.

Homma's 4th Division which was to head the landings was to attack as near as possible to Malinta Tunnel, known to be the core of resistance. But when his barges reached the coast a current sweeping through the North Channel swept them to the eastern end of the island. It was a bright moonlight night and as they drifted helplessly, struggling against the tow, the men on the beaches opened fire. The Japanese, who had anticipated landing without difficulty, now found themselves incurring heavy losses.

As he heard the news Homma became more and more apprehensive. Had he, despite the bombardments, made a terrific miscalculation? However, although he did not then know it, some units had managed to get ashore, including elements of the 61st Infantry Regiment, under Colonel Gempachi Sato.

While the beach defenders were annihilating the second wave of invaders, who were trying to gain a foothold, and believed that landings had been prevented, Sato quietly organised his men and began to advance on Malinta Tunnel. The secrecy of their movements was such that it was not until midnight that Homma learnt there were forces ashore. Even so, the number of Japanese on the island was not more than a thousand men, while the defenders could muster something like 15,000.

Howard immediately ordered a counterattack. But this was not easy to execute. The men who were to make it were in Malinta Tunnel which was packed with some 4,000 to 5,000 people, including civilians, wounded and nurses, so that it was only with the greatest difficulty that they succeeded in getting through it. Furthermore, despite their superiority in numbers, bad communications on the American side made it impossible to assemble forces in the places where they were wanted. Groups which were actually attacked fought with reck-less bravery, but some of those still on the beaches did not know the Japanese had landed until the next morning.

Homma, who had so far heard nothing but reports of casualties and failure and knew that the only force ashore was a small one, heard with horror that the Americans were counterattacking. With their far larger numbers it seemed certain that they must now throw his troops into the sea.

He still had adequate resources of men, but the damage done by the Corregidor shore forces had reduced him to twenty-one landing barges. He was convinced that Corregidor had broken him and told his fellow staff officers: 'I have failed miserably.'

The truth was his troops were on the brink of success. Part of Sato's forces had outflanked the American counterattackers. Some artillery had been landed and brought to the combat area, while three tanks which had also crossed the channel were thrown in at 1000. And it was these which sealed the fate of Corregidor. The defenders now had all their forces committed and there was no longer an opportunity of destroying the Japanese beachhead which was hourly increasing in strength.

At 1030 on 6th May Wainwright – like King before him – took the only decision now open – to surrender. The naval radio station which had been moved to the Rock after the destruction of Cavite came to life for the last time. 'Message for General Homma . . . Message for General Homma,' it kept repeating. At the same time a white flag was run to the top of the highest flagpole and the men were ordered to destroy their weapons.

Meanwhile Wainwright with two of his officers made his way towards the Japanese line, now on Denver Hill, the incline which led to the entrance to Malinta Tunnel. He was to find, however, as King had found, that even surrender itself was not a straightforward matter. The first Japanese officer they met was a lieutenant who passed them on to a colonel. Wainwright insisted that he would surrender only to Homma and after some persuasion the colonel accompanied them by landing barge to Bataan. Here they were taken to what Wainwright later described as a 'dingy white house' and on its terrace waited for Homma's arrival. At one stage they were ordered to go down on to the front lawn to parade for the benefit of Japanese movie cameramen.

They were still standing there when Homma drove up in a shiny Cadillac. He was followed by a second car carrying staff officers and a third with the Japanese war correspondents always in his entourage. Homma, a giant among his fellow officers, stepped from the car, stood for a moment eying the American with what Wainwright called a 'bored contempt', and then brushed past. A long table had been arranged on the porch and here conquered and conquerors faced each other. Homma spoke perfect English, but he had with him his interpreter. Through him he told Wainwright at the commencement of negotiations that he was not prepared to consider any surrender which did not include all the forces in the Philippines – meaning by this, of course, Sharp's troops still holding out in Mindanao.

Wainwright answered that he was only responsible for those on Corregidor. The troops in the Visayas and Mindanao were no longer under his command. Homma, who obviously knew the American command structure, asked suspiciously how long these troops had ceased to be under Wainwright? He was told 'some days', though in fact they had been released only just before he left to cross the lines.

Homma, through his interpreter, said that in that case hostilities would continue until his surrender terms were accepted, and rose from the table followed by his officers.

As he left Wainwright was urged by one of his associates to act quickly lest the troops still defending, and with them the wounded and their nurses in Malinta Tunnel, should be massacred.

Wainwright asked the Japanese colonel who had brought him to Bataan what was to happen now. He answered: 'We will take you back to Corregidor and then you can do what you damn well please.'

Another of Wainright's companions approached the Japanese interpreter and he overhead him say, 'General Wainwright was given the opportunity and he refused it.'

The Japanese colonel told him that in any case as Homma had now left he could surrender only to the commander of the Imperial Japanese Forces on Corregidor itself.

Back on the island, where he found the Japanese had now advanced to the mouth of the caves, Wainwright decided there was nothing for it but to take Sharp's forces back under his command and surrender them. A document incorporating this term was then drawn up and translated into Japanese and at midnight that night, 6th May, Wainwright scrawled his signature across the bottom of it.

By this time the Japanese were more or less in complete control of the tunnel and early in the morning a Japanese colonel strode into Wainwright's room, announcing himself as an emissary from the general staff and from Homma's headquarters, sent to discuss the surrender.

It now remained for Wainwright to take Sharp's forces back into his own control and he therefore dictated a letter to him explaining this and the need for the troops in Mindanao to surrender.

With this act the capitulation of the Philippines was complete and Wainwright himself a prisoner. As the news passed from man to man Malinta Tunnel began to empty and during the next few days the Japanese were carrying out the task of rounding up the 15,000 defenders in the island.

The Last Word

Battles rarely end tidily, and that signature across the surrender document was not quite the final word. In Mindanao, Sharp ignored the call to give in and held on for three more days, his forces facing constantly growing opposition now that the whole weight of the Fourteenth Army could be brought against them. Then on 9th May he radioed MacArthur in Australia his final message: 'Enemy comes through right flank. Nothing further can be done.'

Save for the guerilla war which was to continue until MacArthur made his triumphant and dramatic return in

October 1944, the Philippines campaign was over.

The battle for Luzon, and particularly the stands in Bataan and Corregidor are events which after seeming so immensely significant at the time have ever since been belittled by both American and British historians. The only people who continue to take them seriously are the Japanese. It may now seem to our more dispassionate eyes that they did not have the effect upon the Pacific War they were believed to have had in those day. Nevertheless, in the context of that crisis, the struggle, protracted and brutal as it was, produced a salutary effect on Allied morale. Merely by holding on so doggedly the defenders of the Philippines made manifest that the Japanese were not invincible. Perhaps that was lesson enough.

At the same time it was a lesson learnt almost fortuitously and at great and, in many ways, needless cost.

It would be a rash man who claimed the discernment to unravel all the

A Japanese soldier oversees the work of Filipino citizens

skeins which contribute to success or failure of armies or nations at war. Two factors must always predominate however: chance and human personality. It was not only farsighted planning and audacity which brought the Japanese their early successes, it was also chance – for them lucky, for the Americans tragic. It had been chance, for example, that the massive assault convoys, making their way to Pearl Harbor, were not spotted.

It was chance, too, that aided them in the Philippines. Warning messages that were never delivered, pursuit planes that took off or landed at the wrong moment, anti-aircraft shells that were out-of-date. Even the most sophisticated and civilised of men are at base superstitious and such combinations of chance will lead the members of one side to believe themselvs specially favoured by fate and those of the other to conclude that their 'luck is out'.

It could not, of course, be only misfortune which brought about the greatest defeat American arms have ever known, dwarfing even Appomattox Courthouse.

No one will now know for sure why the B-17s and other aircraft of the Far Eastern Air Force were still on the ground when the Japanese air attacks took place – hours after they were scheduled. Certainly the laws of chance played a part there, too, but so also did the conflict of personalities between the taciturn Sutherland and the more adventurous Brereton.

Yet Sutherland and Brereton were only the supporting players to the central figure of the drama, the USAFFE commander, General Douglas MacArthur. The theatrical metaphor is not accidental. Eisenhower, a former chief of staff to MacArthur was, on one occasion, asked by a young lady if he knew him. He answered: 'Madam, I not only knew him I studied dramatics under him.'

The war in the Philippines is left to the guerrillas

That actor's sense of occasion which MacArthur possessed was in many ways a valuable gift. Brilliant generals have failed to inspire their troops to victory for the lack of it. What the situation of December 1941 needed, however, was a cool, clearly reasoning head and a temperament capable to making decisions without consideration to the effect they would create.

It was not for this reason alone that MacArthur failed in the Philippines. He failed also on more fundamental grounds. If there are clashes of personality among subordinates it is an executive's responsibility to see they do not affect the functioning of the total unit. On this score alone he cannot, try as he might, escape his share of the blame in the destruction of air forces. If, in fact (as he sought to indicate subsequently), decision-making responsibility devolved upon Brereton, why, when he failed so culpably, was he not disciplined? Is not the inescapable conclusion from this, as from the confusion surrounding the orders about attacking Formosa, that someone had something to hide which a deep inquiry would reveal?

Nor is the indictment limited to what happened in the first few hours of hostilities. The questions keep presenting themselves. Why, for example, in view of MacArthur's own urging of an aggressive and dynamic policy, were no plans to implement such a policy ever made? The importance of Formosa to Japanese schemes was well enough known. The long-range, heavy bombers were available. Why were decisions left so late that they inevitably brought only disaster? MacArthur can hardly excuse himself on the ground that he hoped and expected war to be delayed for five months longer. It is, after all, a commander's job to have contingency plans not merely for some future conflict – in conditions more nearly those of his own choosing – but for attack at any given moment, however comparatively unready he may find

POWs at Fort O'Donnell, the
Japanese 'Death Camp

himself. In December 1941 MacArthur appeared to have no such plans.

As Gavin Long points out in *MacArthur as Military Commander*, in the six years he had been in the Philippines he had failed to raise an army of anything like the efficiency required for the task it was going to be called upon to undertake, though both he and Quezon had anticipated what that task was likely to be. When, moreoever, the challenge came, he placed far too great a reliance upon them, instead of relying upon his crack unit, the Philippine Division, which in any case was constantly splintered.

Why, since he claimed to have divined where the Japanese blow would fall, were there no troops on the beaches to meet them? It is here that an invasion force is most vulnerable (weather made the Japanese even more so) and such a chance to turn them back does not recur. The German generals who failed to turn back the Allied Normandy invasion could at least claim they were taken by surprise in the choice of location.

And, allowing for the problems of terrain and the shortage of transport, why was there no mobile force? As the problem of movement had been with them for so long, why had no thought been given to it?

Why was no real and sober attempt made to judge the strength of the Japanese attacks? The debilitating effect upon ill-equipped and untrained defenders of feeling that they were fighting an overwhelming enemy must have contributed enormously to the failure of the Filipinos in battle. Troops under attack almost invariably overestimate the size of the forces confronting them, but such exaggerations are normally adjusted at more senior level. It is hard to understand why experienced officers so constantly made the job for their troops seem harder than it really was.

Why, when it became obvious that this was the only possibility, was the movement of men and supplies to

Above: **Major-General W F Sharp after release from a POW compound.**
Below: **Japanese military commander during the occupation; General Tanaka**

Left: the Japanese flag rises over the conquered Philippine Islands. *Above:* 'I came through, and I shall return'

Bataan so delayed? Why, before the 'sideslip', had no effort been made to establish a real, working Intelligence service? Instead, MacArthur's headquarters were forced to rely on unsubstantiated rumour and barrack-room gossip.

That there was a lack of any sense of urgency among junior officers was obvious even on the first day of war and after the news of the attack on Pearl Harbor was generally known. But this is no excuse in itself. If such a state of mind existed it could only be because senior officers had failed to instill a sense of urgency, perhaps had failed to display it.

Whatever MacArthur achieved later in the Pacific War, round his efforts in the Philippines in 1941 criticisms proliferate until it becomes fatuous to pursue them. In summing up one could say that he fought the Philippines campaign as certain chess players engage in a chess game: having lost all their most powerful pieces in a series of disastrous mistakes they fight tenaciously at the end to avoid being mated. So MacArthur, having been pushed off the main battlefield, resorted to the holding action of Bataan.

What, strategically, he hoped to achieve it is hard to see. 'WPO-III' and its successor 'War Plan Rainbow V' were designed for a war in which the Pacific Fleet would be a major weapon. Even with his small understanding of naval operations he can hardly have hoped to be relieved by sea.

Or was it, perhaps, that his sense of occasion came to his aid once more? All the world loves a game loser. If this was in his mind he calculated well, for by holding out as he did, long after the other, but much smaller Western garrison in South-East Asia had fallen, he made Bataan a byword among the embattled Allies and himself the hero of the hour whom none dared overlook.

Bibliography

The Turn of the Tide Arthur Bryant (Doubleday & Co, New York)
The Philippines Raymond Nelson (Thames & Hudson, London)
Reminiscences Douglas MacArthur (McGraw-Hill Inc, New York)
The Two Ocean War Samuel E Morison (Little Brown & Co, Boston)
MacArthur as Military Commander Gavin Long (Batsford, London)
Philippine Political and Cultural History Gregorio Zaide (Manila)
Kōgun: The Japanese Army in the Pacific War Saburo Hayashi (The Marine Corps Association, Quantico, Virginia)
Pearl Harbor A J Barker (Ballantine Books Inc, New York)